Iconic Albums
Pink Floyd
Dark Side Of The Moon

Richard Ward

DEDICATION

For Avgusta

CHAPTER ONE
THE BAND BEFORE THE ECLIPSE

Pink Floyd's evolution from psychedelia to conceptual mastery

Before they became architects of one of the most enduring albums in music history, Pink Floyd were sonic explorers navigating the shifting tides of London's psychedelic underground. The story of The Dark Side of the Moon begins not with the pulse of a heartbeat or the chime of cash registers, but with a group of Cambridge friends who dared to stretch the boundaries of rock and sound itself.

Formed in 1965 by Syd Barrett, Roger Waters, Richard Wright, and Nick Mason, the band first operated under several names—Tea Set, The Abdabs, and The Spectrum Five—before settling on The Pink Floyd Sound, a tribute to bluesmen Pink Anderson and Floyd Council. But while their name paid homage to the past, their music looked to the future.

In London's swinging mid-60s, they became fixtures at clubs like UFO and Middle Earth, where light shows and extended jams created a hallucinogenic fusion of art, music, and rebellion. Their debut album, The Piper at the Gates of Dawn (1967), captured Barrett's whimsical, kaleidoscopic vision—fairy tales wrapped in reverb and whimsy—but the band's center would soon collapse.

Syd Barrett was more than a frontman—he was the creative nucleus. But as his mental health deteriorated, exacerbated by heavy LSD use and possible undiagnosed schizophrenia, the band faced a crisis. By 1968, David Gilmour had joined to cover for the increasingly unreliable Barrett. Eventually, Syd was out. The light of the early Pink Floyd dimmed, but a new direction emerged.

Barrett's absence left a void, but also a question: what now? With Waters taking the lyrical helm and Gilmour's guitar anchoring the band in a new melodic seriousness, Pink Floyd evolved from psychedelic improvisers into conceptual visionaries.

The post-Barrett era saw a run of albums—A Saucerful of Secrets (1968), Ummagumma (1969), Atom Heart Mother (1970), and Meddle (1971)—that were rich in experimentation but uneven in execution. These were albums full of sprawling ideas: orchestral suites, ambient soundscapes, and sonic oddities like "Several Species of Small Furry Animals Gathered Together in a Cave and Grooving with a Pict."

Yet among the madness, a pattern was forming. Atom Heart Mother flirted with classical arrangements, while Meddle's "Echoes" was a 23-minute journey that demonstrated the band's growing taste for cohesion. These were the rehearsals for something greater.

During this time, Roger Waters' role as conceptual leader grew stronger. His interest in politics, mortality, and the human condition began to dominate lyrical themes. David Gilmour, with his soulful, blues-tinged guitar and understated vocal delivery, became the sonic anchor. Wright's keyboards added space and atmosphere, while Mason's drumming evolved from rudimentary beats into dynamic, mood-driven rhythm.

The band was maturing—less interested in abstract freak-outs and more intrigued by structure, theme, and message.

By 1972, Pink Floyd had outgrown their underground roots. Their live performances had grown increasingly ambitious, with quadraphonic sound systems and early versions of Dark Side tracks already circulating. A new idea had taken root—one that would abandon randomness in favor of narrative, coherence, and meaning.

They weren't just writing songs anymore. They were building albums as architecture—cohesive structures with emotional arcs, philosophical inquiries, and studio wizardry working in harmony.

The groundwork was complete. The Syd Barrett era was over. The whimsical had given way to the existential. The pieces were in place, and the eclipse was beginning.

CHAPTER TWO
STORM CLOUDS FORMING – THE EARLY 1970S

The social, cultural, and political climate surrounding the album

The early 1970s were a time of disillusionment. The optimism of the 1960s had curdled into something more anxious, more cynical. The flowers of peace and love were withering, trampled by economic crises, war, political scandal, and the crushing realization that utopias were fragile dreams. It was in this shifting atmosphere that The Dark Side of the Moon was conceived—not as an escape from reality, but as a mirror to it.

By 1972, the counterculture had lost its halo. The Woodstock generation had aged into the Watergate generation. Charles Manson had stained the hippie movement with blood. Altamont had turned "free concert" into a cautionary tale. Vietnam still raged, even as protests mounted. The Beatles were gone, and the Rolling Stones had taken on a harder, darker tone. The party was over.

Meanwhile, Britain itself was teetering. Inflation and unemployment were rising. Strikes became a regular occurrence. The post-war social contract was beginning to crumble. For many, the future no longer felt like a promise—it felt like a weight.

Pink Floyd, with their growing international presence, stood at a crossroads. They could have chased escapism or fantasy, but instead, they chose something more confrontational: the human condition itself.

Rock music was changing too. Gone were the jangly anthems of youthful rebellion. In their place were heavier, darker sounds—Black Sabbath's doom-laden riffs, King Crimson's technical chaos, and the cerebral textures of prog rock. Albums like Fragile (Yes), Close to the Edge, Selling England by the Pound (Genesis), and Thick as a Brick (Jethro Tull) signaled that the LP format was becoming the new artistic canvas.

But Pink Floyd wanted to do more than dazzle musically—they wanted to say something. Roger Waters, in particular, had grown frustrated with

3

abstraction. He wanted to craft an album that tackled the invisible forces that define our lives: time, money, fear, death, madness.

The Dark Side of the Moon was not the first concept album—The Beatles' Sgt. Pepper, The Who's Tommy, and Frank Zappa's Freak Out! had already broken that ground. But what Floyd would do was refine the idea, giving it clarity and cohesion that hadn't yet been achieved.

They weren't just telling a story—they were mapping out modern existence. The pressures of capitalism, the ticking of mortality, the fracture of mental health—these weren't just themes; they were realities, familiar to anyone coming of age in the 1970s.

Elsewhere, the Cold War cast a nuclear shadow over everyday life. Space exploration had plateaued after the moon landing. The energy crisis loomed on the horizon. Environmentalism and feminism were gaining ground, but the old structures remained rigid. In many ways, it felt as though society had entered a holding pattern—progress had paused, and anxiety had filled the void.

That's what Dark Side tapped into. It was less a protest album and more a philosophical reckoning. It didn't offer solutions, just truths—harsh, poetic, and eerily relatable.

The increasing presence of technology—computers, synthesizers, mass communication—began to shift how people viewed the world and each other. Alienation became a theme not just in literature or film, but in daily life. Machines were encroaching on human spaces, and the notion of individual agency was fading beneath systems too vast to comprehend.

Floyd responded by embracing that very technology: tape loops, synthesizers, quadrophonic sound. Yet rather than letting it replace emotion, they used it to highlight it—to make the mechanical feel human, the impersonal feel deeply personal.

The Dark Side of the Moon didn't emerge in a vacuum. It was the product of a troubled world, crafted by four men standing in the eye of a cultural storm. And instead of shielding their eyes, they opened them— and invited us to do the same.

CHAPTER THREE
ECHOES OF AN IDEA – FROM 'MEDDLE' TO MOON

How "Echoes" laid the groundwork for a new kind of concept album

Before there was The Dark Side of the Moon, there was "Echoes." A single, sprawling track that took up the entire second side of Meddle (1971), "Echoes" was not just a bold musical statement—it was a rehearsal for the unified, atmospheric, and emotionally resonant experience Pink Floyd would perfect one album later. It was the spark that lit the long fuse toward Dark Side.

Meddle represented a turning point in Pink Floyd's creative journey. After several years of post-Syd searching—where albums like Ummagumma and Atom Heart Mother embraced experimentation often at the cost of coherence—Meddle struck a new balance. It was the first time the band sounded focused, collaborative, and grounded in a shared purpose.

Though side one contained shorter songs like "One of These Days" and "Fearless," it was the second side's 23-minute epic, "Echoes," that truly redefined what Pink Floyd was capable of.

"Echoes" wasn't written in one go. It was assembled in pieces: a single piano note from Rick Wright that sounded like a sonar ping; a haunting vocal harmony between Wright and Gilmour; eerie, dissonant guitar effects; sprawling improvisational passages. And yet, when it all came together, it didn't feel fragmented—it felt cinematic, like a guided trip through the ocean depths of the mind.

It had no distinct chorus, no radio-friendly structure. Instead, "Echoes" breathed. It built and receded like waves. It evoked feelings rather than stating them. Most importantly, it told a story—not through lyrics alone, but through sound design, space, and emotional contour.

This was new territory for Pink Floyd. And it would prove essential.

Lyrically, "Echoes" explored themes of connection, communication, and human empathy—"Strangers passing in the street / By chance two separate glances meet." These would become central motifs in The Dark Side of the Moon, as Waters began to probe what divides people—and what unites them.

There were also sonic blueprints: the use of atmospheric keyboards, layered guitar textures, and dynamic shifts in tempo and mood. These elements wouldn't just reappear on Dark Side—they would become the album's very language.

Unlike later Pink Floyd albums, where internal tensions would often fracture the creative process, "Echoes" was a true group effort. Wright's contributions were central. Gilmour's guitar sang more than it roared. Waters focused less on dominating the concept and more on enhancing the mood. Even Mason's drumming took on a painterly quality—restrained yet essential.

This cohesion was key. The band had learned how to listen to one another, to develop an idea organically over weeks of experimentation. That same collaborative spirit would guide them during the earliest rehearsals of Dark Side in 1972.

When Pink Floyd took "Echoes" on the road, it became a centerpiece of their live shows. Performing it night after night gave the band a newfound confidence in crafting immersive experiences. They began to think less like a traditional rock band and more like sound architects, designing entire sonic environments for their audience to step inside.

It was during these performances that the seed of The Dark Side of the Moon was planted—not as a mere collection of tracks, but as a singular statement. One piece. One arc. One message.

Though "Echoes" was a stepping stone, it was never just a prototype. It stands as one of the most beautiful, mysterious, and emotionally expansive pieces in Pink Floyd's catalog. But its legacy is bigger than itself—it taught the band how to reach beyond individual songs and instead build worlds.

With "Echoes," Pink Floyd didn't just hint at what they could do.

They proved it.

CHAPTER FOUR
ABBEY ROAD AND ALAN PARSONS

Studio innovation, sound engineering, and the man behind the console

It's easy to talk about The Dark Side of the Moon in terms of philosophy, concept, or lyrical depth—but behind the ideas was a machine, and at the heart of that machine was a place: Abbey Road Studios. And within its hallowed walls stood a young engineer who would help Pink Floyd capture lightning in a bottle: Alan Parsons.

This wasn't just another rock album—it was a laboratory experiment conducted in one of the most legendary studios in the world. And the lab technician turned out to be a magician.

Abbey Road Studios in London was already the sacred ground of British recording by the early 1970s. The Beatles had transformed its corridors into a sonic playground. It had seen orchestras, choirs, tape loops, and Moog synthesizers long before such things were fashionable.

But while Abbey Road had a reputation for tradition and excellence, it also had another advantage: cutting-edge equipment. And more importantly, staff who weren't afraid to push it to the limit.

This was the perfect setting for what Pink Floyd was attempting—an album that would transcend not just musical genres, but the very limits of recording technology at the time.

At just 24 years old, Alan Parsons had already worked on Let It Be and Abbey Road by The Beatles. He was meticulous, curious, and always looking for ways to do things differently. When he was assigned to engineer Pink Floyd's next album, he didn't just record—it was as if he sculpted sound.

Parsons wasn't afraid to experiment with tape loops, reverb chambers, or unusual mic placements. He didn't treat the studio as a neutral space—

he treated it as an instrument.

In Floyd, he found willing collaborators. This wasn't a band asking for a clean mix—they were asking for sonic architecture.

Parsons helped Floyd craft one of the album's most iconic moments: the cash register loop in "Money." It wasn't a pre-packaged sound effect—it was stitched together from actual coins, tills, paper tearing, and more, all arranged meticulously on tape. It wasn't just a gimmick—it was rhythm, character, and theme in one.

Likewise, the clocks in "Time"? Those weren't sampled from a sound library. Parsons and his team recorded each one live from real grandfather clocks and alarm clocks, triggering them simultaneously in the studio for the perfect chaotic impact.

Parsons' attention to detail—and willingness to record things the hard way—gave Dark Side a tactile, almost physical presence. These weren't abstract sounds. They were felt.

One of the band's early requests was to create an immersive, surround-sound experience. Parsons was instrumental in adapting the mix for quadraphonic sound, a new (and largely impractical) format that placed listeners in the center of the music.

Though quadraphonic playback systems didn't catch on, the principles behind them—spatial design, layered movement, and the illusion of three-dimensional audio—remained baked into the album. Even in stereo, Dark Side feels like it surrounds you. That's no accident.

Parsons wasn't officially a member of Pink Floyd, but his influence on the album is impossible to ignore. From the heartbeat that opens "Speak to Me" to the way Clare Torry's vocals were recorded for "The Great Gig in the Sky," his fingerprints are everywhere.

Ironically, Parsons never received a Grammy for his work on the album, and though he later achieved fame with The Alan Parsons Project, his name often remains in the shadow of the band.

But for Floyd fans and audiophiles, Parsons is a hero—the technician who made the impossible sound real.

The final mix of The Dark Side of the Moon—meticulously crafted in Studio Three—was a triumph of sonic layering. Voices drift in and out like memories. Instruments shift across channels like ghostly apparitions. The album feels alive—because it was recorded by people who treated every sound like a living thing.

Abbey Road was the vessel. Parsons was the architect. Pink Floyd was the visionary. Together, they didn't just record an album.

They built a world.

CHAPTER FIVE
THE CONCEPTUAL FRAMEWORK – LIFE, DEATH, AND MADNESS

Roger Waters' thematic vision that ties the whole album together

If The Dark Side of the Moon had only been a collection of brilliantly produced songs, it would still have earned a place in music history. But what elevated it into legend—what made it the eternal heartbeat of rock music—was its unflinching, unified exploration of what it means to be human. And at the center of this journey was Roger Waters, the band's bassist and emerging conceptual visionary.

This wasn't just an album about time, or money, or madness. It was about all of it—interwoven into a seamless meditation on existence itself.

By 1972, Waters had begun assuming creative control of Pink Floyd's direction—not through ego, but through focus. Where earlier albums had dabbled in surrealism or sprawling abstraction, Waters wanted something precise—a statement with teeth.

Inspired by the pressures he felt in his own life—fame, mortality, disconnection—Waters envisioned a suite of songs bound by a simple yet profound idea: the forces that quietly crush us. Not the grand traumas of war or heartbreak, but the everyday machines that grind us down: time, greed, mental illness, fear, conformity, and death.

From the very first sound of a heartbeat in "Speak to Me," the album announces its purpose: this is about being alive. But life, for Waters, is not a linear path—it's a cycle. One that begins with wonder and ends in entropy.

The album's structure follows this circular arc:

- Birth and innocence in "Breathe"
- Anxiety and chaos in "On the Run"
- The finite march of time in "Time"
- The final surrender in "The Great Gig in the Sky"

- Temptation and corruption in "Money"
- Separation and judgment in "Us and Them"
- Mental collapse in "Brain Damage"
- Total eclipse in "Eclipse"

Thematically, it's a life lived—and lost—in 43 minutes.

Waters was writing about everyone, but he was also writing about himself. His growing unease with fame, his introspection about his father's death in WWII, and his observations of former bandleader Syd Barrett's mental deterioration all fed into the album's DNA.

The song "Brain Damage," for instance, is not just about madness in the abstract—it's about Syd, about the fear of becoming him, about the thin line between genius and psychosis. "Time," meanwhile, speaks to Waters' own existential dread—how youth slips away unnoticed until it's too late to change course.

The genius of Waters' writing lies in this duality: it's intimate, yet somehow global. Every listener hears themselves in it.

Unlike many albums of its era, Dark Side doesn't point fingers or raise fists. It doesn't rage at governments or preach solutions. It simply holds up a mirror and says: this is the machinery we're trapped in. It doesn't scream—it confesses.

There's no character or narrative thread to follow. Instead, there are themes—emotional signposts that build toward a devastating crescendo. The darkness Waters paints is not external. It's inside you. The dark side of the moon is the part of the soul we hide, or forget, or deny.

Waters didn't just write lyrics—he conceptualized how everything should connect: sound effects, song order, vocal snippets, transitions. Interviews with roadies and crew members were recorded and interwoven between songs, their musings on death, violence, and fear creating an eerie stream of subconscious thought.

It's not storytelling. It's internal monologue. Waters didn't want you to follow a character's journey. He wanted you to feel your own.

What makes Dark Side so powerful is that despite its heaviness, it isn't hopeless. There is beauty in its despair. There is grace in its resignation. Waters doesn't scream "The world is broken!"—he whispers, "So are we. And that's okay."

In "Eclipse," the final track, Waters offers the album's single, shining truth:

"And everything under the sun is in tune / But the sun is eclipsed by the moon."

It's a line that feels both tragic and strangely comforting. The darkness isn't out there. It's in all of us. And acknowledging it is the first step toward light.

With Roger Waters' vision as its spine, The Dark Side of the Moon became something far rarer than a rock record. It became a philosophical ritual—a meditation on the pressures that bind us, and the fragile consciousness we use to resist them.

Next up would come the tracks themselves—each one a shard of the greater whole.

CHAPTER SIX
SPEAK TO ME – THE SOUND COLLAGE THAT BEGINS IT ALL

A study of tension, heartbeat, and anticipation

Before a word is spoken, before a note is played, there is a heartbeat.

The Dark Side of the Moon doesn't open with melody—it opens with biology. It opens with life. And with that single, pulsing throb, Pink Floyd makes their mission clear: this album isn't just about sound—it's about existence. "Speak to Me," the wordless prologue to one of the most celebrated albums of all time, lasts barely a minute. But in that minute, it tells you everything you need to know.

This is no overture. It's a summons.

The first sound we hear—soft, distant, and growing—is a heartbeat, created using a kick drum run through heavy processing. It is both literal and symbolic. It grounds the album in something human, something physical. We are not in the clouds. We are in the body.

Gradually, fragments begin to appear: the whoosh of a cash register, the maniacal laughter of road manager Peter Watts, Clare Torry's soaring vocal wail, the ticking of clocks, the scream from "The Great Gig in the Sky." None of these sounds belong to "Speak to Me" alone—but they are all part of the album's memory.

This is Dark Side's DNA, spliced and scattered like memories in a dream before consciousness kicks in.

Nick Mason, the band's drummer, is the sole credited composer for "Speak to Me." It's a rare moment where the often-overlooked member takes a lead. His role wasn't about instrumental dominance, but curation. Mason constructed the track by compiling snippets from the rest of the album—a sonic preview of what's to come.

The title is ironic. No one sings. No one plays a melody. Instead, it's an invitation: Listen closely. The album is about to speak—but in its own language.

"Speak to Me" doesn't just preview the songs—it sets the tone. The album won't start with comfort. It starts with tension. The heartbeat grows louder. The sounds overlap. Laughter becomes unsettling. Screams echo in the distance. There's a sense that something is about to happen—something profound, maybe terrifying.

It's suspense in pure audio form, and it leads directly into "Breathe (In the Air)" with no pause. When that first chord finally washes in, it feels like relief, like waking from a nightmare into calm daylight.

That's the genius of "Speak to Me." It doesn't ask you to understand. It asks you to feel.

Though only a minute long, "Speak to Me" encapsulates the album's core technique: using fragments to build cohesion. These aren't disconnected sounds—they're thematic links. The cash register (greed), the clocks (time), the scream (death), the laughter (madness)—each one a tile in the album's mosaic.

Roger Waters once described Dark Side as an "expression of political, philosophical, and humanitarian empathy." "Speak to Me" is that empathy in raw form—a swirl of human experiences colliding before language gives them meaning.

As "Speak to Me" dissolves into "Breathe," the transition is seamless. But it's not just a musical segue—it's a thematic birth. The heartbeat that opened the album has delivered us into life. The murk gives way to clarity. Sound becomes song. Experience becomes reflection.

You don't start listening to The Dark Side of the Moon.

You are born into it.

CHAPTER SEVEN
BREATHE (IN THE AIR) – PHILOSOPHICAL CALM

A song of existential warning dressed in tranquil beauty

The heartbeat fades. The screams subside. And then—like a sunrise over a long night—comes "Breathe."

The album's first true song, "Breathe (In the Air)" enters with warmth, space, and serenity. Its lush chords and gliding pedal steel guitar invite the listener into a moment of peace. But listen closer, and the calm begins to unravel. Behind its meditative surface lies a quiet warning: life moves faster than you think, and if you don't take control, it will take control of you.

This is Pink Floyd at their most deceptive—inviting you to relax while gently pointing out the futility of the rat race.

David Gilmour's guitar glides across the mix like clouds, shaped by reverb and sustained bends on his pedal steel. Rick Wright's organ work drifts in like breath itself—cyclical, constant, soothing. The tempo is unhurried, almost drowsy. The production is air itself—open, fluid, inhaling and exhaling.

Yet that very openness feels empty, too. There's something haunting in its calmness, something detached. We are not celebrating peace—we are questioning what we do with it.

It's not psychedelic in the sense of wild experimentation. It's psychedelic in restraint—a song that opens the mind through atmosphere rather than excess.

Roger Waters' lyrics are minimal but weighty. The very first lines establish the tone:

"Breathe, breathe in the air / Don't be afraid to care."

It sounds like advice from a guru, or perhaps a parent. But quickly, the tone shifts:

"Run, rabbit, run / Dig that hole, forget the sun."

What begins as nurturing turns into criticism—you're running in circles, digging yourself into a meaningless life. The rabbit, a traditional symbol of innocence, becomes a corporate drone.

Waters isn't preaching—he's observing. This is the silent panic of modern existence: the pursuit of progress without reflection, the mechanical motions of adulthood replacing true living.

"Long you live and high you fly / But only if you ride the tide."

It's conditional. Your freedom depends on compliance. And even then, "balanced on the biggest wave," you're not surfing—you're waiting to die.

David Gilmour's vocal delivery is key. He sings not with anger, but with a kind of weary kindness. There is no snarl, no sarcasm—just acceptance. It's as if he already knows the listener won't heed the advice. He's not trying to change minds. He's offering perspective.

This is what makes "Breathe" so affecting: it doesn't rage against the machine. It looks you in the eye and gently says, You're already in it.

Musically and thematically, "Breathe" establishes one of Dark Side's most powerful motifs: the illusion of control. The music loops. The lyrics warn. The sound seduces. But it's all part of a trap—comfortable, familiar, inescapable.

That trap is life without intention. Existing without awareness. Running without direction.

"Breathe" isn't trying to wake you up with a scream. It's trying to show you you're already asleep.

Depending on how you listen, "Breathe" can be heard as the album's philosophical invitation, or its emotional goodbye. It introduces every theme that will follow: time, conformity, greed, madness, mortality. And yet, it already seems to suggest that it's too late.

The song doesn't build. It doesn't evolve. It simply exists—just like the people it describes.

CHAPTER EIGHT
ON THE RUN – TECHNOLOGY, TERROR, AND TRANSIT

Tape loops, synths, and the fear of flying

There are no lyrics. No verses. No chorus. And yet "On the Run" speaks volumes.

In just over three and a half minutes, Pink Floyd created a sonic panic attack—an aural embodiment of modern anxiety. It's the sound of movement without purpose, technology without control, and fear without escape. Nestled between the contemplative breath of "Breathe" and the existential weight of "Time," "On the Run" serves as the album's nerve centre—its pulse quickened, its hands trembling.

What you're hearing isn't just a song. It's the inside of a mind in meltdown.

The heart of "On the Run" is the EMS Synthi AKS, a briefcase-sized analog synthesizer that, in the hands of Pink Floyd, became a time machine, a bomb, and a hallucination all at once.

Roger Waters and David Gilmour programmed the sequence—a frantic, looping rhythm that feels like both a race and a trap. There's no melody, just relentless propulsion. The sound never rests. There's no room to breathe. It's techno-paranoia, years before techno existed.

This was radical in 1973. Where most rock bands used synthesizers for embellishment, Floyd used one to replace the band entirely. Guitar, bass, and drums disappear. The machine takes over. The result is alienating—

but that's the point.

The concept behind "On the Run" began with Roger Waters' own fear of flying. The band had grown accustomed to international travel, but for Waters, air travel was a source of dread—not just for its danger, but for its helplessness. Once you're airborne, you're no longer in control. You're just… waiting.

This fear became metaphor. "On the Run" isn't just about airports. It's about the modern condition—the daily panic of schedules, machines, obligations, and the gnawing sense that something could go wrong at any moment.

The track includes actual airport announcements, footstep samples, and an ominous voiceover. Add in distorted laughter, echoing footsteps, and a swelling sense of doom, and the result is unmistakable: paranoia made music.

Midway through the track, a sound like a jet engine rises, screaming across the mix before a massive explosion. It's a horrifying moment—abrupt, jarring, and final. But it's not really about a plane crash. It's about mental collapse.

This is The Dark Side of the Moon's first major emotional rupture. Where "Breathe" lulled us into passive existentialism, "On the Run" rips that comfort away. There's no serenity here. Just forward motion toward the inevitable.

The listener isn't flying anymore. They're falling.

"On the Run" marked a turning point not only for Floyd, but for rock music as a whole. It showed that synthesizers weren't just tools—they could be characters. The track has no lyrics, but it says something: about our relationship with machines, with progress, with fear.

There's a mechanical quality to the rhythm, but also something human—a kind of nervous twitching behind the circuitry. It's the sound of a man trying to keep pace with a world that never stops moving.

"On the Run" was revolutionary in its use of tape loops, a technique where sounds are physically spliced and looped on reels to repeat. It required painstaking precision. But Floyd didn't use this just to show off—they used it to immerse. To trap the listener.

Live versions of the track would evolve with elaborate light shows and quadraphonic sound, often leaving audiences bewildered. It wasn't a song to sing along with. It was a ride—one you couldn't get off.

"On the Run" is motion without meaning, speed without control, fear without form. And as it crashes into the ticking clocks of "Time," we're forced to confront the very thing we've been running from.

CHAPTER NINE
TIME – THE ANTHEM OF MORTALITY

Clocks, solos, and the inevitability of aging

There are no warnings. No lead-ins. Just clocks—dozens of them—striking at once in a chaotic burst of mechanical urgency. It's jarring. It's unignorable. And it's deliberate. With that opening clang, Pink Floyd grabs the listener by the shoulders and delivers the album's most devastating message: your time is running out.

"Time" is not just a song. It's a reckoning. A wake-up call. A lament for years wasted and the realization that the future doesn't wait for anyone.

The now-iconic clock introduction wasn't sourced from a sound effects library—it was recorded by Alan Parsons in a real antique shop, with each chime triggered individually. When stacked together, they created a wall of time—a claustrophobic rush of alarms, reminders, and bells that refuse to be ignored.

It was more than a gimmick. It was a statement. Time isn't a gentle stream. It's an ambush.

And from this chaos emerges one of the greatest rhythm guitar intros in rock: a slow, tribal build-up led by Nick Mason's rototom-heavy drums, driving the track toward something monumental.

Lyrically, Roger Waters captures a universal human panic—the sudden awareness that life has already started. The opening lines, sung by David Gilmour in a voice heavy with resignation, cut deep:

"Ticking away the moments that make up a dull day
You fritter and waste the hours in an offhand way…"

These aren't accusations. They're confessions. The song captures a uniquely modern anxiety: not that death will come too soon, but that it will come without us ever really having lived.

The most haunting line in the song isn't about dying. It's about missing the point of life entirely:

"And then one day you find / Ten years have got behind you…"

It's not death that's frightening. It's lost time.

Gilmour's delivery is weary, raw, and restrained. He doesn't howl—he surrenders. His voice carries the weight of realization, not rebellion.

And then comes the guitar solo—a soaring, aching cry that ranks among the greatest in rock history. It's not technically complex, but it says everything. You can feel the years slipping by in each note—regret, anger, longing, surrender.

It's a solo that doesn't want to end. But of course, it must.

When Roger Waters enters in the bridge—his only lead vocal on the track—his voice is more vulnerable, more wounded. It's a rare moment where the band's lyrical architect speaks directly. And he doesn't sound like a rock star. He sounds like a man realizing his own fragility:

"Every year is getting shorter / Never seem to find the time…"

The words are simple. But that's what makes them brutal. Waters has no interest in cleverness here. He's telling the truth.

The track ends with a reprise of "Breathe", now reframed with hindsight. The warm melody returns, but now it feels more empty. The message is clear: you were warned. But you didn't listen.

The reprise isn't comforting. It's damning.

"Far away across the field / The tolling of the iron bell…"

The field could be freedom—or a graveyard. Either way, the bell tolls for all.

What makes "Time" remarkable is its emotional restraint. There's no melodrama. No sentimentality. Just facts. You are aging. You have wasted time. You will die. But Pink Floyd delivers this with grace, not judgment.

It's not too late, the song seems to say.

But it will be soon.

With "Time," The Dark Side of the Moon confronts the listener directly. No more metaphors. No more soft entry points. It dares you to ask: What are you doing with your one precious life?

CHAPTER TEN
THE GREAT GIG IN THE SKY – WORDLESS EMOTION

Clare Torry's vocal improvisation and the song's spiritual release

After the clocks of "Time" fall silent and the dust of mortality begins to settle, the listener is not given answers—but elevation. The Great Gig in the Sky is not a song in the traditional sense. It is a release. A cry. A prayer. A surrender.

It is also one of the most astonishing moments in all of rock music—a track that transcends language, genre, and form, carried almost entirely by a single human voice.

Clare Torry didn't sing lyrics. She sang life leaving the body.

At first, the track feels like an elegy. Rick Wright's gentle piano chords float upward like incense in a cathedral. There is calm, but also grief. The atmosphere is funereal, yet not morbid—it's reverent.

Fragments of dialogue surface in the mix, taken from interviews with roadies and crew. One voice mutters, "I'm not afraid of dying... anytime will do." It's not said with fear—it's said with peace. Death isn't portrayed as horror. It's inevitable, even beautiful.

Then the voice comes in.

Not words. Not lyrics. Just pure, human emotion, delivered by a then-unknown session singer named Clare Torry, who would etch her name into eternity in under three minutes.

Torry was called in at the last minute—just another day's work at Abbey Road. She had no guidance other than, "sing something emotional." What she delivered was something between gospel, opera, and a spiritual exorcism.

In one improvised take, Torry captured the arc of dying: panic, resistance, acceptance, and release.

She begins with a restrained moan, but it quickly escalates—crying, wailing, gasping. It's childbirth in reverse. Her voice becomes a conduit for everything unspeakable about death. And yet, it never becomes grotesque. It remains musical, controlled, divine.

Torry later confessed she felt embarrassed about the session, as if she'd overdone it. But when the band heard it, they knew instantly: this was it. The song no longer needed lyrics.

The voice had said it all.

What makes "The Great Gig in the Sky" so singular is how much it communicates without saying anything. In an album obsessed with what pressures us—time, greed, madness—this track simply lets go.

There is no critique here. No concept. Just experience. Death, rendered not as a wall, but as a doorway.

The fact that this moment of raw transcendence was achieved through improvisation only enhances its mystery. You can't script this. You can't plan for truth.

Rick Wright's contributions to The Dark Side of the Moon are often underappreciated, but here, he is the silent architect. His piano line is both melody and mood, oscillating between major and minor chords as if unsure whether to mourn or rejoice.

The arrangement gives Torry space, but not emptiness. The music never competes—it supports. This is musical empathy at its most refined.

Placed at the end of Side A, "The Great Gig in the Sky" functions like an intermission—a moment to step outside the cycle of fear and reflect on its end. After the mechanical dread of "On the Run" and the regretful urgency of "Time," this track floats above the battlefield like a soul leaving the body.

It doesn't promise heaven. It doesn't threaten hell. It simply says: This is what passing sounds like.

Torry was originally paid a flat session fee and left uncredited for years. But in 2004, she sued for co-authorship—and won. The credit now reads "Wright / Torry," as it always should have. Her voice is not an embellishment. It is half the song.

What she gave Pink Floyd was not a performance. It was immortality.

"The Great Gig in the Sky" is more than music—it's release. It's a moment of surrender on an album about control, a breath taken before Side B plunges into the harsh realities of the modern world.

CHAPTER ELEVEN
MONEY – THE SOUND OF GREED

7/4 time, cash registers, and biting sarcasm

If Side One of The Dark Side of the Moon ended in death, then Side Two opens with rebirth—straight into the fluorescent glow of a supermarket, a bank vault, a shopping mall, or an accountant's office. Welcome back to Earth. Welcome to "Money."

Here, Pink Floyd shifts gears. Gone are the philosophical abstractions. In their place: commerce, consumerism, and cold, hard cash. But if you think this track is just a critique of capitalism, think again. It's not a protest song. It's a satirical portrait—clever, cynical, and catchy enough to make you tap your foot while it robs your soul.

This is the sound of greed—and the band knew it too well.

The song opens with a now-iconic tape loop of cash registers, coins dropping, paper tearing, tills opening. Each sound is perfectly placed in 7/4 time—an odd, lurching rhythm that never quite lets you settle in.

Roger Waters stitched this intro together by hand, manually cutting tape segments into a continuous loop. It's a rhythm born from machines, but it grooves like something human—unnerving, hypnotic, and unrelentingly precise.

Then the band kicks in. Nick Mason's drum groove locks tight with Roger Waters' funky bassline, and suddenly we're in uncharted territory: Pink Floyd has written a hit single in 7/4 time.

David Gilmour, often known for his restrained and melodic style, cuts loose here with some of the grittiest blues rock of his career. His guitar tone snarls with distortion and sarcasm. The solo in the middle section, especially after the band shifts briefly into a more conventional 4/4, is electric—furious, slick, and oddly danceable.

"Money" isn't delicate. It's not poetic. It's swaggering, cynical, and slightly drunk on its own success.

Just like the system it mocks.

Roger Waters' lyrics are knife-sharp satire. Sung by Gilmour with deadpan cool, they present the voice of a person completely sold on the virtues of wealth:

"Money, it's a crime / Share it fairly, but don't take a slice of my pie."

It's not a condemnation. It's a confession—an admission of complicity in a system everyone complains about, but no one escapes.

Waters once said he saw "Money" less as a sermon and more as dark comedy. It isn't preaching—it's mirroring. The line "I'm all right, Jack, keep your hands off my stack" is as British in its sarcasm as it is universal in its sting.

It's a song about everyone else's greed—until you realize it's also about yours.

Ironically, "Money" became Pink Floyd's first hit in the US—an anthem of greed released by a band on the cusp of extreme wealth and fame. In later interviews, the band would reflect on the strange paradox: they'd written an anti-capitalist song that made them millionaires.

The tension between message and outcome gives "Money" even more weight. It is the system. The song knows it. You know it. And yet… it slaps.

Alan Parsons' engineering once again elevated the track. The panning of the cash register loop, the dry drum mix, the layered guitar tones—it's a technical marvel. Listen on headphones, and the sonic details multiply: the echoes, the tightness of the rhythm section, the clarity of the vocals amidst the chaos.

There's also the subtle layering of voices, returning to the theme of the album's hidden narrators. Roadies and crew members chime in with offhand remarks about wealth and power, giving the track a sense of surveillance—as if greed is always being watched, but never judged.

Despite its complexity, "Money" became a mainstay of classic rock radio—a track that grooves hard enough for casual listeners while offering enough depth for deep thinkers. Its unusual time signature was masked by its funkiness. Its cynicism was masked by its fun.

And in doing so, Pink Floyd achieved something few others have: they made a protest song that you can dance to—without realizing it's about you.

"Money" is not the sound of rebellion. It's the sound of succumbing. But with a wink. And a guitar solo.

CHAPTER TWELVE
US AND THEM – WAR, DIVISION, AND EMPATHY

A ballad that confronts humanity's contradictions

After the cynical snarl of "Money," The Dark Side of the Moon does something remarkable—it softens. Not in impact, but in tone. "Us and Them" is not a scream of protest or a sneer of superiority. It is a lament. A slow, sweeping, mournful meditation on the senseless divisions that define human existence.

This is not a song of revolution. It is a song of recognition—recognition that every war, every border, every "us" and every "them" is a line drawn in sand. And when the tide comes in, all we're left with is loss.

"Us and Them" is arguably Pink Floyd's most beautiful song—musically lush, emotionally weighted, and haunting in its restraint.

Rick Wright's jazzy piano chords float like drifting smoke. Dick Parry's saxophone solo enters not with bravado, but with heartbreak—its phrasing like someone struggling to speak through tears. Gilmour's guitar is understated, almost hesitant. And his vocal delivery? Calm. Cold. Observational.

There's no shouting here. Just a voice watching humanity from a distance—numb, disappointed, exhausted.

"Us and them
And after all, we're only ordinary men…"

The line hits like a whisper in a war zone.

Roger Waters crafts the verses like a series of vignettes—short, devastating glimpses into conflict:

"Forward he cried from the rear
And the front rank died…"

The futility of war is laid bare in two lines. No names. No politics. Just the absurdity of sending men to their deaths while shouting from safety. It's timeless—and damning.

Elsewhere:

"Down and out, it can't be helped but there's a lot of it about…"

This isn't empathy. It's indifference dressed as pragmatism. The kind of callous phrase you hear from someone who's learned to look away from suffering. Waters doesn't blame. He observes. And it's this detachment that makes it hurt more.

There is no villain in "Us and Them." That's the tragedy.

We all are.

The song's title says it all. Us and them. The binary that drives so much of human conflict—nation vs. nation, rich vs. poor, black vs. white, powerful vs. powerless. Yet Waters doesn't hammer the message. He drifts through it, as if stunned by how little has changed across time and history.

The song is universal, but also deeply personal. It asks listeners to question the divisions in their own lives. Who have you called "them"? Who have you dismissed as "other"?

Musically, "Us and Them" moves like a tide. The verses are soft and slow, but then the chorus erupts—a sudden wall of harmony and drums:

"Black! And blue!
And who knows which is which and who is who?"

This moment of musical violence—still beautiful, but urgent—is one of the most effective uses of dynamic contrast in rock history. It mimics the pattern of conflict: long periods of stillness, interrupted by sudden, devastating bursts of chaos.

And then, just as suddenly, it recedes.

Like war itself.

"Us and Them" doesn't offer solutions. It barely offers commentary. Instead, it asks. Are we really so different? Do we even know why we fight anymore?

It's a song that feels like it's trying to remember something important—but keeps forgetting. As if empathy is just out of reach.

Even the fade-out feels like resignation. The voices return, muttering disconnected fragments about violence and morality. One man shrugs, "With... without. And who'll deny it's what the fighting's all about?"

It's not a punchline. It's a mirror.

Where most albums build to a climax with noise, "Us and Them" builds to one with emotion. It is the slow bleed at the center of Dark Side. The moment where the album stops spinning and simply stares—not at society, but at you.

In "Us and Them," Pink Floyd didn't just write a song—they wrote a confession on behalf of all mankind. And as it fades into the surreal abstraction of what follows, it leaves behind a lingering ache:

We are all ordinary men.

And yet, somehow, still at war.

CHAPTER THIRTEEN
ANY COLOUR YOU LIKE – SONIC ABSTRACTION

Instrumental freedom and the improvisational spirit

After the emotional devastation of "Us and Them," The Dark Side of the Moon does something unexpected: it lets go. It stops speaking. It stops mourning. It stops explaining. And instead, it floats into a vivid, wordless landscape of sound. No lyrics. No narrative. Just colour—whatever shade your mind can imagine.

"Any Colour You Like" is the album's great abstraction. A moment of improvisational freedom inside an otherwise carefully composed structure. It's not an interlude. It's not filler. It's the sound of consciousness disintegrating—and the closest the album comes to psychedelia in its purest form.

The track opens with a kaleidoscope of synthesizers—arpeggiated pulses sweeping across the stereo field, created using EMS VCS 3 and Synthi AKS synthesizers. These are not melodic lines. They're waves—textures that shimmer and morph like ripples in a dream.

Then Rick Wright's organ joins, grounded but cosmic. And finally, the rhythm section enters, with Gilmour's guitar gliding in like a comet tail. There are no sharp edges here. Everything glows.

It's not chaos. It's controlled hallucination.

Unlike much of The Dark Side of the Moon, which is tightly arranged and conceptually rigorous, "Any Colour You Like" is rooted in jam session energy. It evolved in live performances long before the album was recorded, allowing each band member space to experiment.

David Gilmour takes the spotlight with one of his most fluid, expressive solos—looped through a Uni-Vibe and delay effects to create cascading harmonies. His guitar doesn't solo in the traditional sense. It paints.

The phrasing is bluesy, but the tone is interstellar. His lines bend, echo, and shimmer—more emotion than virtuosity. It's as if his instrument has forgotten it's a guitar, and instead become a voice without language.

"Any Colour You Like" is the only purely instrumental track on the album (aside from "Speak to Me"), and its placement is crucial. After the heavy themes of war, greed, and mortality, the listener needs release. Not intellectual release. Sensory release.

It's a moment to stop thinking and start feeling. To process all that's come before—not through analysis, but through absorption.

The title itself is a wry allusion to consumer choice—a reference to Henry Ford's famous quote about the Model T:

"You can have it in any colour, so long as it's black."

In other words, freedom of choice is often an illusion. But here, Pink Floyd turns the phrase on its head. This isn't about limitation. This is about limitlessness.

Pick a colour. Any colour. It's your mind now.

Musically, "Any Colour You Like" acts as a bridge—both structurally and emotionally. It connects the emotional devastation of "Us and Them" to the psychological unraveling of "Brain Damage." The track builds tension and then dissolves it, preparing us for the album's final descent.

And like many moments on Dark Side, its transition is seamless. It doesn't start—it emerges. It doesn't end—it evaporates.

This is Floyd's genius: songs don't stand alone. They breathe into each other.

Despite its looseness, "Any Colour You Like" is not without structure. The chord progression follows a consistent loop, and the improvisation stays tethered to a clear emotional arc. This is freedom within form—a sonic metaphor for the album's larger themes.

You may feel like you're choosing your path, but the structure is already in place. You're not outside the system.

You're inside it—and dreaming.

"Any Colour You Like" is Pink Floyd's invitation to wander. It doesn't ask you to understand. It asks you to feel. It is music made of mist, colour, and memory—a brief moment where the boundaries of the album disappear, and you're left floating in the dark.

CHAPTER FOURTEEN
BRAIN DAMAGE – THE LOONIE INSIDE

Mental illness, Syd Barrett's shadow, and lyrical power

If The Dark Side of the Moon has a beating heart, "Brain Damage" is it—and that heart is cracked. After the soaring abstraction of "Any Colour You Like," the album returns to words, to form, to madness. This is the moment when the carefully controlled themes of mortality, time, greed, and isolation finally collapse under the weight of their own pressure.

And through that collapse, Roger Waters steps into the spotlight—not just as a songwriter, but as a confessor. "Brain Damage" isn't a portrait of someone else's insanity. It's a mirror held up to the listener's own fragile mind.

This is where the loonie lives.

Though never mentioned by name, "Brain Damage" is widely—and rightly—understood to be about Syd Barrett, the band's founding member whose mental decline in the late 1960s forced his departure.

Barrett had once been Floyd's spark: whimsical, brilliant, unpredictable. But by 1968, he had unraveled, overwhelmed by psychedelic drug use and, possibly, schizophrenia. His absence haunted the band, especially Waters, who often described Barrett as a casualty of modern life's inability to handle visionary minds.

"And if the dam breaks open many years too soon…"

It's a reference to psychic collapse—Barrett's, and perhaps their own.

"Brain Damage" is not mocking. It is not diagnosing. It is mourning. Waters isn't laughing at the loonie on the grass—he's acknowledging him. And maybe envying his freedom.

This is one of Roger Waters' defining vocal performances. His voice doesn't try to impress—it communicates. It's theatrical, yes, but also conversational. He's telling you something important, something personal:

"The lunatic is on the grass
The lunatic is on the grass…"

The image is innocent at first—someone breaking societal rules, trespassing on public space. But soon, it gets darker:

"The lunatic is in the hall
The lunatics are in my hall…"

The division between "them" and "me" dissolves. The lunatic has moved inside.

"And if the cloud bursts, thunder in your ear
You shout and no one seems to hear…"

It's a scream for help in a soundproof world.

Musically, "Brain Damage" walks a delicate line between lullaby and breakdown. Rick Wright's Hammond organ hums gently beneath the melody, while Gilmour's backing vocals add a layer of ghostly calm. The structure is simple, almost hymn-like, but it slowly intensifies, building toward something bigger.

By the final chorus, the song swells—not with chaos, but clarity. It's the kind of climax that feels like a revelation, not an explosion.

You understand now: the madness isn't outside. It's within.

Throughout Dark Side, Waters toys with the idea that madness is not an illness, but a response—a reaction to the unbearable pressures of modern life: aging, capitalism, war, fear. "Brain Damage" is the culmination of that argument.

We are not mad because we're weak. We go mad because we're human.

And madness may not even be the worst fate. The lunatic on the grass may be the only person who sees the truth.

As the song draws to a close, the final line lands like prophecy:

"And if the band you're in starts playing different tunes
I'll see you on the dark side of the moon…"

It's not a threat. It's a reassurance. A message to Barrett. To the band. To us.

If you break, you're not alone.

There's a place for you.

"Brain Damage" is the moment The Dark Side of the Moon drops its mask. It stops being philosophical and becomes intimate. It's not about society anymore. It's about you. It's about what happens when the pressure becomes too much, and the cracks start to show.

CHAPTER FIFTEEN
ECLIPSE – EVERYTHING UNDER THE SUN

A climactic resolution and universal truth

The storm has passed. The lunatic has spoken. The voices have faded. And now, Eclipse rises—not as a closing statement, but as a cosmic summation. This is not just the final track of The Dark Side of the Moon—it is its thesis. A brief, explosive, soul-rattling piece that gathers every thread of the album's narrative and binds them into one final, all-encompassing truth.

In just over two minutes, Roger Waters delivers his gospel. Not of salvation, but of totality. Everything you've heard—the clocks, the screams, the saxophones, the madness, the money, the breath—is here.

Everything under the sun.

And the sun is eclipsed by the moon.

Musically, "Eclipse" is simple. A repeating, ascending chord progression, rooted in E major, layered with choir-like harmonies and rising intensity. It has the grandeur of a religious ceremony, yet none of the dogma. It's uplifting. It's ominous. It's final.

As Rick Wright's organ swells and Nick Mason's drums pulse with a steady, heartbeat-like cadence, David Gilmour and Roger Waters alternate vocals, blending seamlessly in tone and intent. Their voices no longer sound like individuals—they sound like humanity.

There are no verses, just declarations.

"All that you touch
And all that you see
All that you taste
All you feel…"

It's a catalog of human experience—basic, primal, universal. There's no room left for abstraction. This is everything.

Line by line, Waters builds a list of what it means to be alive:

"All that you love
All that you hate
All you distrust
All you save…"

These aren't philosophical musings. These are facts. Lived realities. The song doesn't tell you what to feel. It reminds you that you feel. It insists: You are here. You are alive. You are part of this.

And then it crescendos:

"And everything under the sun is in tune…"

For a moment, it sounds like resolution. Everything fits. Everything is working. Everything has purpose.

But then—the turn:

"…but the sun is eclipsed by the moon."

This single line casts a shadow over all that came before. All that you touch, all that you see—is in darkness. The moon, symbol of madness and the subconscious, has blocked out the light. The implication? No matter how much we love, strive, feel, or build… there is always a shadow. Always an unknown. Always a side we cannot see.

It's not nihilism. It's not despair. It's acceptance.

Waters isn't saying nothing matters. He's saying everything does—even the darkness.

As the music fades, we hear a faint voice—barely audible:

"There is no dark side of the moon, really. Matter of fact, it's all dark."

It's a closing paradox. Spoken by doorman Gerry O'Driscoll, it suggests that our obsession with division—light versus dark, sane versus insane, us versus them—is missing the point. We're all in the dark, trying to make sense of it. And that's what unites us.

Not the answers.

The questions.

"Eclipse" doesn't explode. It concludes. It doesn't seek redemption. It observes. And in doing so, it offers the most honest ending an album like this could have.

Not with hope.
Not with fear.
But with truth.

You are not alone.

You are everything.

And the dark side? It's not a place. It's part of you.

Eclipse is the final breath of The Dark Side of the Moon, but its impact echoes forever. It doesn't close a door—it opens one. The listener is left not with resolution, but with reflection. The album may end, but the questions it asks never do.

And that's why, decades later, we're still listening.

CHAPTER SIXTEEN
LYRICS THAT SPEAK UNIVERSALLY

Roger Waters' words and the human experience

The success of The Dark Side of the Moon is often attributed to its sonic innovations, production brilliance, and musical cohesion. But strip away the soundscapes, the tape loops, the stereo wizardry—and what remains? Words.

And not just clever words, or poetic ones—universal ones.

Roger Waters' lyrics on The Dark Side of the Moon aren't written in code. They don't require footnotes or philosophical background. They speak in a language everyone understands: mortality, madness, time, money, fear, connection. These aren't rock star problems. These are human problems.

And that's what makes the album timeless.

Waters doesn't rely on metaphor for its own sake. There are no dragons, no political slogans, no indulgent riddles. His genius lies in clarity. He writes as though speaking to a friend, delivering hard truths gently—as if he's already lived them.

Take "Time":

"And then one day you find
Ten years have got behind you."

It doesn't get more direct than that. No adornment, no embellishment—just the creeping horror of life slipping by unnoticed. Everyone understands that moment. Everyone has felt it.

Or "Us and Them":

"With, without / And who'll deny it's what the fighting's all about?"

It's a single line that captures the futility of war, politics, and division better than volumes of theory. Waters makes you feel the absurdity by understating it.

This is lyrical empathy—not superiority. Waters isn't talking down to his audience. He's talking with them.

One reason these lyrics resonate across cultures, generations, and languages is because they bypass specificity. "Money" isn't about a particular economy. "Breathe" isn't about a particular religion. "Brain Damage" isn't about a particular diagnosis. They're all about the human condition—the sense that we're born into a machine we never built, racing against a clock we never set.

These lyrics don't judge. They observe. They give voice to thoughts we've all had, but never said aloud:

- I'm scared of wasting my life.
- I feel like I'm going mad.
- I'm working hard, but I don't know why.
- I'm afraid of dying.
- I just want to be seen.

Waters captures these with surgical precision—but also warmth. His lyrics ache with recognition.

Many of Waters' lines are repeated—mantras, maniacal chants, circular thoughts:

"All that you touch / All that you see..."

"Run, rabbit, run..."

"The lunatic is on the grass..."

This repetition is intentional. It mimics the obsessive thinking of modern life—the loops we get stuck in. It also helps etch the words into the listener's mind, turning them into truths. You don't just hear the lyrics— you remember them. They become part of your inner monologue.

Even when writing about deeply personal subjects—like Syd Barrett's mental decline in "Brain Damage," or his own existential dread in "Time"—Waters avoids indulgence. He doesn't wallow. He translates his experience into language others can claim as their own.

In doing so, he bridges the gap between artist and audience. He reminds us that no matter how private our fears may feel, we are not alone in them.

Part of the lyrical magic of Dark Side lies in its voice—not just Waters', but the voices woven throughout the album: doormen, roadies, wives, strangers. They speak plainly, sometimes absurdly, sometimes profoundly:

"I've been mad for f***ing years…"

"I'm not afraid of dying. Anytime will do."

These voices don't act as background. They add texture to the lyrics, creating a world where every opinion matters—even the offhand ones. Waters knew that a philosophical album needed grounding. And what better grounding than real people?

Roger Waters wrote these lyrics in his late twenties. That alone is staggering. But what's more remarkable is how they continue to resonate—decade after decade, across changing times, shifting politics, and evolving music trends.

Because no matter how the world changes, some questions remain:

- What am I doing here?
- Is this all there is?
- Is everyone else feeling this too?

Waters' answer is both devastating and comforting: yes.

In a world where so much lyrical writing feels designed to impress or obscure, Waters' work on The Dark Side of the Moon stands as a testament to a deeper kind of power—truth spoken clearly, with courage and compassion.

CHAPTER SEVENTEEN
THE ART OF THE ALBUM – STORM
THORGERSON'S PRISM

How the cover became an icon of rock imagery

Before a single note plays, before the heartbeat pulses, before the clocks strike—you see it. A black void. A white beam. A triangle. A sudden explosion of colour. No title. No band name. Just a prism splitting light.

The cover of The Dark Side of the Moon is one of the most recognisable images in popular culture. It is not just an album cover. It is a symbol— of mystery, perfection, introspection, and the infinite.

But what's most remarkable is how little it says—and how much it means.

This is the genius of Storm Thorgerson, the visual architect behind Pink Floyd's most enduring image.

In 1973, album covers were often cluttered with psychedelic illustrations, band portraits, and loud typography. But Pink Floyd—and Storm Thorgerson—wanted something different for The Dark Side of the Moon. Something that reflected the album's clarity and thematic depth.

Thorgerson, a founding member of the design collective Hipgnosis, understood that restraint could be more powerful than noise. He presented several ideas to the band, but the moment he showed them the prism design, drawn by fellow artist George Hardie, the decision was unanimous.

It was immediate. Just like the cover itself.

At first glance, the image seems purely scientific: a beam of white light enters a prism and refracts into a rainbow spectrum. But in the context of the album, it becomes something more profound.

The white light is life—undifferentiated, unexamined, pure. The prism is the human experience—the mind, the pressures of time and greed and madness. And the colours? The full spectrum of being. Everything we feel. Everything we become.

It's a visual metaphor for the entire record.

Life enters. It passes through you. And it fractures into everything under the sun.

There's also a subtler layer: order and chaos. The input is linear. The output is wild. The Dark Side of the Moon is about that very transition— from control to collapse, from clarity to complexity.

And perhaps most hauntingly, the prism sits in blackness—space. The unknown. The dark side.

One of the most daring decisions was to omit the band's name and album title entirely from the front cover. This wasn't arrogance. It was confidence.

Pink Floyd understood that the artwork spoke for itself. It didn't need explanation. It didn't need branding. The image was already iconic before the first record even spun.

And in doing so, they redefined the possibilities of album art. This wasn't just packaging. It was visual philosophy.

Thorgerson didn't stop with the cover. The gatefold sleeve featured a dramatic live performance photo—bathed in red light, faceless, cosmic. The inner sleeve included heartbeat imagery, lyrics, and further graphics expanding the prism motif.

There were also posters and stickers included in the original vinyl release—making the physical record a full experience, not just an object.

This approach would become standard in the years to follow, but at the time, it was revolutionary.

The prism design quickly escaped the vinyl sleeve and entered pop culture at large. It became a poster in bedrooms. A badge of identity. A tattoo. A T-shirt worn by generations of teenagers who hadn't even heard the full album—but felt something when they saw the image.

You don't need to know anything about Pink Floyd to recognise the prism. And that's why it works. It's not just marketing—it's mythology.

Thorgerson would go on to design many more covers for Pink Floyd—Wish You Were Here, Animals, Division Bell—as well as artwork for Led Zeppelin, Genesis, and Muse. But the Dark Side prism remained his masterpiece.

He once said:

"You don't give them what they want—you give them what they didn't know they wanted."

That's what the prism did. It gave people an image for something they'd only ever felt. A way to visualise confusion, fear, beauty, and transcendence—all without a single word.

The music of The Dark Side of the Moon changed how albums were heard. Storm Thorgerson's cover changed how they were seen. Together, they proved something timeless:

Great art doesn't explain.

It invites.

CHAPTER EIGHTEEN
SYNTHS, LOOPS, AND INNOVATION

The technology that gave Dark Side its futuristic edge

Pink Floyd didn't just write songs—they sculpted sound. On The Dark Side of the Moon, technology wasn't just a tool for polish. It was a central character, shaping the emotional tone and driving the conceptual depth of the album. From the hypnotic pulse of "On the Run" to the surreal sonic collage of "Speak to Me," this was music engineered with precision, not just played.

In 1973, no other rock band was doing what Floyd was doing in the studio. While others still saw recording as a means of capturing live performance, Pink Floyd treated the studio as an instrument in itself—and in doing so, they built the future.

The most defining technological sound of Dark Side is the synthesizer—used not to replace instruments, but to create sounds that had never been heard before.

Two key machines shaped the album:

- EMS VCS 3
- EMS Synthi AKS

Compact, modular, and notoriously tricky to tame, these British-made synths were revolutionary. They didn't just create tones—they created landscapes. Waters and Gilmour used them not just for melody, but for texture, ambience, and atmosphere.

On "On the Run," the entire track is built around a sequenced loop on the Synthi AKS. That pulsating, frantic rhythm—mimicking the panic of air travel and modern life—was painstakingly programmed step by step. It was mechanical and emotional at once.

This wasn't background decoration. It was narrative sound design.

Before digital sampling, Pink Floyd were building complex tape loops manually—cutting, splicing, and threading magnetic tape through reels in real time. These loops became the rhythmic heartbeats of the album.

The most famous example is the cash register loop in "Money." Roger Waters recorded individual sounds—coins clinking, receipts tearing, tills slamming—and strung them into a perfect 7/4 rhythm. It was musique concrète repurposed for rock.

Likewise, the ticking clocks in "Time" were recorded by engineer Alan Parsons in a clock shop, each chime triggered live and layered into a surround-sound explosion. Nothing was "off the shelf." Everything was built.

These loops weren't gimmicks. They were ideological tools—representing capitalism, time, mechanisation, and chaos. And they made Pink Floyd sound like nothing else on Earth.

Pink Floyd were pioneers in exploring quadraphonic sound—an early form of surround audio. Though only a few listeners ever heard the quad mix, its influence was baked into every stereo version of the album.

Tracks were mixed with a sense of motion: sounds panned across channels, voices whispered from unseen corners, footsteps walked from speaker to speaker. It wasn't just stereo—it was cinematic.

The effect was immersion. You didn't just listen to Dark Side—you entered it.

Even the vocals were treated with technological flair. On "Us and Them," for example, Gilmour's voice is processed with subtle echo and reverb, giving him an almost ghost-like presence—detached and observational. On "Brain Damage," Waters' voice sits close and dry in the mix, heightening the sense of madness whispering in your ear.

Clare Torry's performance on "The Great Gig in the Sky" was recorded dry, but then layered, compressed, and balanced with almost surgical precision. It wasn't about auto-tuning—it was about letting the human voice hit supernatural heights through careful design.

While the band conceived the sound, Alan Parsons executed it. His role as engineer was instrumental—he brought patience, creativity, and technical daring. His background with Abbey Road and Let It Be made him fluent in both traditional and experimental studio methods.

Parsons knew how to make analog tape machines do things they weren't designed to do. And his attention to detail helped Floyd pull off some of the most ambitious production ideas of the decade—without losing clarity or cohesion.

His reward? He didn't win a Grammy. But he earned immortality.

The genius of The Dark Side of the Moon is that none of this technology feels like technology. It doesn't get in the way. It serves the emotion.

The synths don't sound robotic. They sound human. The loops don't sound mechanical. They sound symbolic. The effects don't distract. They reveal.

This is the difference between using gear to show off, and using gear to say something that instruments alone can't express.

Pink Floyd chose the latter—and changed the possibilities of what an album could be.

The tools behind Dark Side weren't just cutting-edge. They were soul tools. Tools to shape not just sound, but feeling. And by mastering them, Pink Floyd didn't just craft a sonic masterpiece—they created a world.

CHAPTER NINETEEN
RICK WRIGHT'S FORGOTTEN BRILLIANCE

The often-overlooked atmospheric genius behind the soundscape

In the history of Pink Floyd, three names tend to dominate the conversation: Roger Waters, the conceptual architect and lyrical mind; David Gilmour, the emotive guitarist and iconic voice; and Syd Barrett, the tragic original spark. But quietly, patiently, and perhaps most crucially, Richard Wright was there all along—the soul of the sound.

The Dark Side of the Moon is, in many ways, Rick Wright's most powerful yet subtle contribution to the band's legacy. He was not the loudest member. He was not the most outspoken. But his fingerprints are everywhere—etched into the textures, moods, and sonic atmosphere that make the album timeless.

Wright didn't need to take centre stage.

He built the stage.

Wright's keyboard work is not flashy. It doesn't leap out of the mix. Instead, it surrounds you, fills the space between the notes, and gives the album its emotional depth. He wasn't just playing chords—he was painting environments.

On "Breathe," his Hammond organ and Fender Rhodes electric piano shimmer like sunlight through clouds, giving the track its drifting, dreamlike texture. On "The Great Gig in the Sky," his gospel-infused chord progression on piano becomes the emotional canvas for Clare Torry's unforgettable vocal performance.

And on "Us and Them," perhaps his most stunning moment, Wright crafts a harmonic landscape of melancholy and grace. His jazz-informed voicings elevate the track beyond rock, giving it the feel of a late-night lament for humanity itself.

This wasn't background music.

This was the emotional architecture of the album.

Rick Wright understood something many musicians never learn: what not to play. His use of space and silence was just as deliberate as his notes. His parts never crowded the mix—they enriched it.

He didn't fight for attention. He played for the song. And that discipline allowed the album to breathe—especially in an age where progressive rock often leaned toward overplaying.

His textures weren't designed to impress. They were designed to make you feel something—even if you couldn't quite explain what it was.

Wright also contributed vocals to the album, though his voice is often mistaken for Gilmour's. The two had a similar timbre, and their harmonies throughout Floyd's discography blended with eerie precision.

On Dark Side, Wright's harmonies elevate "Time" and "Us and Them," giving those choruses a ghostly, aching quality. His voice is felt more than heard—another layer in the emotional fog.

Technologically, Wright was deeply involved in shaping the band's sound. He was the band's earliest adopter of synthesizers, and his use of the EMS VCS 3 and Synthi AKS was crucial to the spatial illusion and mood shifts of the album.

On "Any Colour You Like," his synth solos intertwine with Gilmour's guitar in a psychedelic dance—two instruments, one mind. On "On the Run," his eerie pads and textures anchor the panic. And on "Brain Damage," his organ swells rise like distant memories—half-religious, half-hallucinogenic.

Wright made machines sound human. Or maybe, he made humanity sound like a machine quietly falling apart.

Wright's brilliance was rarely loud, and history tends to favour bold statements. He wasn't the conceptual leader. He wasn't the frontman. And in the later years, as tensions with Waters grew, his contributions were downplayed—sometimes even erased.

He was briefly fired during The Wall sessions, reduced to a salaried session musician in the band he helped build. But even then, when he returned for The Division Bell, it was his ambient textures that re-grounded the band's sound.

History may have sidelined him.

But the music never did.

Without Rick Wright, The Dark Side of the Moon would have been colder, flatter, and far less transcendent. His playing isn't what you hum. It's what you feel. He was the emotional resonance of the band—the dusk light behind the silhouette.

If Waters gave us the questions, and Gilmour gave us the voice, Rick Wright gave us the space in which those questions could echo.

He was the prism's glow.

The breath beneath the words.

The genius who whispered where others shouted.

CHAPTER TWENTY
GILMOUR'S GUITAR – TONE, TECHNIQUE, AND EMOTION

The solos that shaped generations of guitarists

David Gilmour doesn't shred. He doesn't dazzle with speed or overwhelm with volume. He communicates. His playing is not about showing off—it's about saying something. And on The Dark Side of the Moon, his guitar becomes more than an instrument. It becomes a voice—a narrator of emotion, a translator of what can't be said in words.

Across the album, Gilmour's solos don't erupt—they emerge. And when they do, they leave a mark not just on the songs, but on the soul of anyone listening. There's a reason why guitarists the world over still study his phrasing, tone, and restraint.

Because Gilmour didn't just play guitar.

He felt it into being.

Perhaps more than any guitarist of his generation, Gilmour developed a signature tone—instantly recognisable, infinitely expressive. It's thick but airy, bluesy but spatial, smooth but emotionally raw.

His rig on The Dark Side of the Moon included:

- A Fender Stratocaster (often black)
- A Hiwatt DR103 amplifier
- Binson Echorec delay unit
- Uni-Vibe, fuzz, and wah effects
- A meticulous ear for EQ and compression

But gear alone doesn't explain Gilmour's tone. His magic lies in his fingertips—his control of vibrato, bends, and dynamics. Every note breathes. Every phrase lingers just long enough to mean something.

It's not about how many notes. It's about how true they sound.

Few solos in rock history are as emotionally loaded as the one in "Time." After verses filled with regret and existential dread, Gilmour's guitar steps forward—not to scream, but to ache.

Each note feels measured, wounded, tired. There's no rush. No flurry. Just sustained emotion, bent to breaking point. He doesn't need words. The solo says it all:

You waited too long.
Life passed you by.
And now… you feel it.

It's not just technically masterful. It's empathetic.

On "Money," Gilmour gets funky—but with teeth. The song's unusual 7/4 time signature challenges the groove, yet Gilmour owns it, weaving blues licks through a rhythm that constantly threatens to trip him.

Then, during the 4/4 break, he lets loose. His solo is biting, distorted, filled with controlled aggression. Yet it still carries structure. There's storytelling in the phrasing—rising tension, climax, release. Like a financial bubble expanding… and bursting.

On this instrumental, Gilmour and Wright trade phrases in a psychedelic jam that feels more like painting than playing. Gilmour's tone here is drenched in modulation and delay, cascading in layers. It's joyful, almost playful—his fingers dancing, the notes sliding like liquid across the track.

It's the most "free" he sounds on the album. And yet, his control is absolute.

Gilmour's voice and guitar often reflect each other—melodically and emotionally. His vocals are calm, clear, and subtly expressive. His solos are the emotional release those vocals suppress. He speaks with poise and sings with logic—but his guitar cries when the words end.

This duality gives The Dark Side of the Moon much of its power. Waters' lyrics challenge you. Gilmour's solos console you.

Perhaps Gilmour's greatest lesson to guitarists is that restraint is strength.

He knows exactly when not to play. He uses silence as punctuation. He makes space speak.

Unlike many of his contemporaries, he never lets technique override message. You never get the sense he's trying to prove anything. He's just... communicating—one note at a time.

And that's why his solos age so well.

They don't belong to a trend or a genre.

They belong to feeling.

Ask any guitarist—from John Frusciante to David Bowie to The Edge—and they'll tell you: Gilmour changed the way we think about guitar tone, emotional storytelling, and the role of the lead player.

On Dark Side, he doesn't just solo.

He narrates.

He reflects.

He feels for us when we can't feel for ourselves.

In David Gilmour's hands, the guitar wasn't a weapon. It was a mirror. And on The Dark Side of the Moon, it reflected not ego or excess—but humanity.

CHAPTER TWENTY-ONE
THE RELEASE – MARCH 1973

Launch day, initial reviews, and early fan reactions

On 1 March 1973, something shifted in the musical landscape—not with a bang, but with a heartbeat.

The Dark Side of the Moon arrived quietly. No grand press conference. No pyrotechnics. Just a jet-black cover, a cryptic prism, and ten tracks recorded by a band more known for extended live jams and psychedelic experiments than commercial ambition. And yet, by the end of that month, it was clear: this album was different. This was not just a release.

It was an event.

In a year when glam ruled the charts and hard rock dominated radios, a cerebral concept album about time, madness, money, and death was hardly a sure bet. Even the name—The Dark Side of the Moon—felt mysterious, ambiguous, even ominous. There was no band name on the cover. No photo. No hype.

Just a pulse and a promise: something extraordinary waits inside.

This kind of artistic confidence was unheard of.

And it worked.

The album charted almost instantly in both the UK and the US. In America, it debuted at #95 on the Billboard 200. Within weeks, it climbed—and it never really left. By the end of 1973, it was a fixture in the top ten. And then it just... stayed. Week after week. Year after year.

It would eventually log over 950 weeks on the Billboard chart, a record so absurd it barely sounds real. At its core, this was an underground band with a cult following. But the record connected with everyone—hippies, audiophiles, stoners, intellectuals, and casual listeners alike.

Why?

Because Dark Side didn't just speak—it understood.

Initial reviews were mixed—not negative, but cautiously impressed. Some critics sensed its greatness, while others couldn't quite grasp what they were hearing.

Melody Maker praised its "musical maturity," but didn't yet call it a masterpiece. Rolling Stone admired its ambition, but seemed more interested in comparing it to previous Floyd efforts. It wasn't immediate praise. It was curiosity.

But over time, the reviews caught up with the audience. And by the year's end, The Dark Side of the Moon was being called what it is today: a landmark in modern music.

For fans, the experience was visceral. Those who dropped the needle and listened all the way through—preferably in the dark, preferably with headphones—emerged changed.

It wasn't an album that asked for applause.

It asked for reflection.

People didn't just like Dark Side. They absorbed it. It became part of their identity, part of their worldview. In dorm rooms, living rooms, bedrooms, cars, and headphones across the world, Pink Floyd wasn't just playing music. They were conducting therapy.

Internally, the success was overwhelming. The band members had no idea it would hit this hard. Suddenly, they were rock royalty. But rather than celebrating, they responded with wariness, introspection—even distance.

Fame didn't suit Pink Floyd. In many ways, The Dark Side of the Moon had already warned them what was coming. The themes of the record—alienation, pressure, madness—were about to become real.

And in that sense, the album wasn't just prophetic for listeners.

It was prophetic for the band itself.

The release of The Dark Side of the Moon marked the moment Pink Floyd crossed over. They were no longer a cult band. No longer just part of the progressive rock underground.

They were now cultural philosophers in musical form—speaking not to a generation, but to the human condition itself.

It didn't happen with a single. It didn't happen with a marketing campaign.

It happened because the music was true.

CHAPTER TWENTY-THREE
FLOYD GOES GLOBAL – INTERNATIONAL REACH

How the album resonated beyond the UK and US

Pink Floyd were, in origin and temperament, a very British band—formed in London, steeped in Cambridge introspection, and shaped by post-war anxieties and English restraint. Their references were cerebral. Their humor, dry. Their influences, drawn from avant-garde jazz, classical minimalism, and the swinging London underground.

And yet, somehow, The Dark Side of the Moon didn't just cross borders. It obliterated them.

This was not just a transatlantic success. It was a global transmission—a message from the subconscious that resonated equally in São Paulo, Stockholm, Sydney, Seoul, and Soweto. The album didn't need cultural translation because it dealt in human constants: time, fear, money, madness, death.

Dark Side was never local. It was cosmic.

In the UK, the album was embraced almost immediately—entering the charts at #2 and quickly rising to the top. In the US, it began its legendary run on Billboard, becoming the sleeper hit of the decade. But the real story was how the album permeated everywhere else.

- In Japan, it was hailed for its precision and production, aligning with the country's emerging audiophile culture.
- In South America, particularly Brazil and Argentina, the album became an underground soundtrack for political reflection and generational alienation.
- In Europe, from France to Germany to the Netherlands, it found a place among the continent's growing progressive rock scene and countercultural enclaves.
- Even behind the Iron Curtain, cassette copies and bootlegs circulated in secret—proof that emotion and message could transcend language and ideology.

It was art that moved not because of marketing but because of magnetism.

Pink Floyd never relied on lyrical storytelling in the traditional sense. Their music was rooted in emotion, space, and symbolism—qualities that didn't require fluency in English. Instrumental passages like "Any Colour You Like" or the moaning catharsis of "The Great Gig in the Sky" spoke in tones that needed no subtitles.

You didn't need to know what "the lunatic is on the grass" meant. You felt it.

You didn't need to analyse the metaphor of an eclipse. You understood the shadow.

The band tapped into something that bypassed culture and went straight into the nervous system.

Storm Thorgerson's now-legendary cover design—a beam of light splitting through a triangle—also played a vital role in the album's global recognition. It was instantly recognisable in any language, any region, any record shop.

It looked scientific and spiritual. Modern and ancient. Western and universal.

Even people who had never heard the album could identify it. In remote corners of the world, the prism became a flag—not of a country, but of a shared internal experience.

Translations of Pink Floyd's lyrics—often unofficial—circulated in fanzines and liner notes across dozens of countries. Yet many listeners didn't even require them. They played the record as ritual, not as story.

In some countries, Dark Side was associated with meditation. In others, rebellion. In some places, it was even used in classrooms to teach English, audio engineering, or existential philosophy. In every case, the record was relevant—adopted and adapted by the local culture, without losing its essence.

Though the band's touring was heavily focused on the UK, US, and parts of Western Europe during the early 1970s, their influence far outpaced their physical presence.

Bootlegs of The Dark Side of the Moon live shows were prized throughout Asia, South America, and Eastern Europe. Floyd's meticulous light shows and quadraphonic sound were legendary by reputation alone—mythic performances that many fans would only dream of seeing.

But even without seeing Floyd live, the impact was tangible. The album inspired musicians across genres—Brazilian psych-rockers, German electronic pioneers, Eastern Bloc underground acts—all tracing their ambition back to Dark Side's sonic boundary-breaking.

Pink Floyd didn't just tour the world. They echoed through it.

And The Dark Side of the Moon became more than a record. It became a shared interior language—spoken in silence, in headphones, in late-night dorm rooms and roadside cassette decks, in cities and villages and countries that could not have been more different... yet all understood.

Because some music doesn't need translation.

It just needs to resonate.

CHAPTER TWENTY-FOUR
SYD BARRETT'S LINGERING INFLUENCE

Madness, creativity, and legacy

He wasn't in the room.
He didn't write a note.
He never played a single chord on The Dark Side of the Moon.

And yet, Syd Barrett is everywhere.

His presence haunts the record like a phantom—unseen but deeply felt. In every whisper about madness, in every scream of anxiety, in every question about time and the self, there is the unmistakable shadow of Pink Floyd's original leader. The Dark Side of the Moon is not about Syd Barrett.

But it cannot exist without him.

Syd Barrett was more than just the band's first frontman—he was their founding vision. With his whimsical, surreal songwriting and experimental approach to sound, Barrett shaped Pink Floyd's earliest identity. The Piper at the Gates of Dawn (1967) is almost entirely his— a kaleidoscopic blend of Lewis Carroll fantasy, psychedelic improvisation, and childlike wonder.

But the same imagination that made him a genius also made him fragile. By 1968, Barrett's mental health was deteriorating rapidly, worsened by heavy LSD use and what may have been undiagnosed schizophrenia. His behavior became erratic. Performances collapsed. Communication broke down. Eventually, the band—reluctantly—had to let him go.

He drifted into obscurity. But his absence became a wound the band never stopped feeling.

Where Piper had celebrated fantasy and escape, Dark Side confronted the real world—cold, relentless, inescapable. In many ways, the two albums represent opposite poles of the same soul: innocence versus awareness, joy versus anxiety, creation versus collapse.

But Syd's influence didn't vanish with his departure. It mutated.

Roger Waters in particular became obsessed with the question that Syd had embodied:

What happens when a brilliant mind can't survive the pressure of the world?

That question sits at the centre of The Dark Side of the Moon—in "Brain Damage," in "Time," in the album's very heartbeat. The record is not a biography. It is a reckoning.

Waters' line in "Brain Damage" is often taken literally, and for good reason:

"The lunatic is on the grass…"

This is not a cartoonish depiction of mental illness. It's a coded cry for Syd—the mad genius watching from the margins, uncontainable, uncared for, misunderstood. The line that follows is even more revealing:

"And if the dam breaks open many years too soon…"

A metaphor for mental collapse. And an acknowledgment that Syd's fall wasn't just tragic—it was premature, and perhaps preventable.

Waters would later describe Dark Side as an album about things that "make people mad"—time, work, stress, money. But behind all of that, the subtext was clear:

Syd didn't go mad in a vacuum.
He was a casualty of the system.

Although Syd Barrett was still alive in 1973—living quietly, withdrawn from public life—The Dark Side of the Moon functions in part as an emotional eulogy. Not just to Syd as a person, but to the idea of pure creativity unprotected by the world.

It's a record that constantly asks: How do we keep going when the

brightest among us burn out?
And: How much of ourselves do we lose by trying to survive?

Syd had chosen—or been forced—to opt out.

The rest of the band had opted in.

But they never forgot what it cost him.

Barrett's influence on Dark Side wasn't musical. It was moral. His absence shaped the album's perspective—its empathy, its anxiety, its need to understand the edge.

He became a symbol for all that is unruly, unquantifiable, and unguarded in human life.

In many ways, the record's heartbeat is his—not in rhythm, but in spirit.

That's why listeners who know Barrett's story feel him in every corner of the album. And why those who don't... still sense something tragic humming underneath.

Long after The Dark Side of the Moon, the band would return to Barrett more directly. Wish You Were Here (1975) was written explicitly as a tribute. But Dark Side is more nuanced. It doesn't name him. It doesn't dramatize him. It carries him—gently, painfully, with guilt and awe.

He is the unspoken "you" in every question.

He is the lunatic, the dreamer, the casualty, the muse.

He is the prism's missing color.

CHAPTER TWENTY-FIVE
THE LIVE EXPERIENCE – FROM WEMBLEY TO THE MOON

How the band brought the album to life on stage

The Dark Side of the Moon was never meant to stay on vinyl.

From its very conception, it was a performance piece—a continuous, thematic experience designed to be heard as one uninterrupted journey. Before the album had a title, before it had lyrics, it had already been performed live, road-tested, and reshaped by Pink Floyd on stage.

It didn't just debut in a studio.

It debuted under lights, in fog, in sound that swirled around the audience like a dream breaking apart.

And once the album was released, Pink Floyd turned its live presentation into something legendary—a fusion of music, theatre, and immersive spectacle that pushed the limits of what a rock concert could be.

The first full performance of the album—then working-titled Eclipse (A Piece for Assorted Lunatics)—was held at The Dome in Brighton on 20 January 1972, more than a year before its official release. Audiences heard early versions of songs like "Breathe," "Time," and "Us and Them" before they were fully recorded.

The idea of testing new material live was unusual, even risky. But for Pink Floyd, it was essential. The band treated the stage as a laboratory, refining the transitions, tweaking arrangements, and using the audience's reaction as a barometer.

By the time they entered Abbey Road to record, The Dark Side of the Moon was already a live creature.

One of the definitive early post-release performances took place at London's Wembley Empire Pool in November 1974. With its imposing architecture and massive crowds, Wembley became the perfect setting for Pink Floyd's growing ambition.

Here, Dark Side wasn't just performed—it was delivered like a sacred rite.

The band played the entire album in sequence, uninterrupted, as a singular piece. Lights were synced to sound. Films projected behind them. Smoke drifted like thought. Quadraphonic sound filled the venue, surrounding listeners in clocks, screams, and heartbeats.

There were no speeches. No banter.

Just immersion.

Bringing The Dark Side of the Moon to life on stage required more than musicianship—it required innovation. Floyd were among the first bands to tour with quadraphonic PA systems, enabling sound to move around the audience in real time.

They used:

- Click tracks and backing tapes, rare at the time, to keep complex loops in sync.
- Custom lighting rigs that responded dynamically to musical changes.
- Projection screens showing surreal visuals, from abstract film loops to lunar landscapes.
- Pyrotechnics and sound effects precisely timed to dramatic moments ("On the Run's" explosion, for instance, became a recurring climax).

This wasn't a gig. It was a sonic theatre production.

And audiences weren't dancing or shouting—they were absorbing, many of them seated, silent, transfixed.

Pink Floyd were never showmen in the traditional sense. Onstage, they were still, almost invisible in the shadow of their own sound. But that detachment worked in their favor. It gave the performance an aura of mystery—as though the music were coming not from a band, but from the cosmos itself.

The musicians were precise:

- Gilmour, delivering note-perfect solos, cool and composed.
- Wright, hidden behind keyboards, crafting textures in real time.
- Waters, focused, intense, sometimes narrating.
- Mason, keeping time like a heartbeat in the dark.

They weren't rock stars. They were conduits.

As Dark Side gained momentum, the live show became a global event. From the US to Europe to Japan, Floyd brought the album to venues large and small, building a reputation as the most ambitious live act of their era.

Fans didn't just attend—they remembered.

Decades later, concertgoers still recall hearing the first heartbeat echo through the PA... the clocks crash into "Time"... Clare Torry's scream in "The Great Gig in the Sky" brought to life by a live vocalist.

These weren't just concerts.

They were experiences etched into memory.

Even after the band moved on to new projects, The Dark Side of the Moon remained a cornerstone of their live identity.

- In 1994, Pink Floyd performed it in full during the Division Bell tour.
- Roger Waters toured it globally from 2006 to 2008.
- And in 2023, to mark its 50th anniversary, a new round of tributes, performances, and reissues brought the album back to the stage for a new generation.

Every performance is slightly different. But the essence never changes.

Because Dark Side was never just an album.

It was, and still is, a live ritual—performed not for applause, but for recognition.

CHAPTER TWENTY-SIX
COVER VERSIONS AND TRIBUTES

From Easy Star All-Stars to Dream Theater—homages and experiments

Some albums are played.
The Dark Side of the Moon is interpreted.

To cover a song is one thing. To cover an entire album—especially one as seamless, sacred, and sonically complex as Dark Side—is a rare act of both courage and devotion. And yet, generation after generation of artists have returned to it, not to imitate but to dialogue with it.

Each tribute becomes a kind of translation—filtered through genre, era, and culture. From reggae collectives to progressive metal bands, from jazz orchestras to lo-fi indie producers, Dark Side has become a musical Rorschach test—open to infinite reinterpretation.

Because once an album becomes universal, it becomes everyone's.

Perhaps the most famous—and most daring—reinterpretation is Easy Star All-Stars' Dub Side of the Moon, a complete reimagining of the album through the lens of reggae and dub. Clock ticks become echo chambers. Basslines are slowed, stretched, submerged.

What could have been novelty became revelation. Critics and fans were astonished by how well the themes of disorientation, capitalism, and existential angst translated into Jamaica's deepest grooves. Even the spoken word samples were re-recorded with a Jamaican accent, retaining the original's surreal quality while giving it new cultural resonance.

The album became a cult hit, leading to live tours and multiple reissues.

It proved Dark Side didn't belong to one sound.

It belonged to human feeling.

If Easy Star All-Stars brought Dark Side into the world of dub, Dream

Theater launched it into the outer reaches of prog-metal. Their 2005 live performance of the entire album (recorded at Hammersmith Apollo) was executed with clinical precision and virtuosic flair.

For Dream Theater, this was pilgrimage through technique—every solo, every transition, every vocal passage meticulously recreated, sometimes with added complexity. It was less reinterpretation than reverence through reconstruction.

Yet their performance captured the emotional thrust too—reminding audiences that precision need not sacrifice power.

It was a tribute by scholars. And it worked.

- The Flaming Lips, in collaboration with Stardeath and White Dwarfs, released a psychedelic and chaotic version of Dark Side in 2009. Their approach: deconstruct to honor. It was noisy, warped, and divisive—but undeniably bold.
- The Royal Philharmonic Orchestra and others have rendered orchestral versions that emphasize the album's cinematic qualities—"Time" as overture, "Us and Them" as a sweeping lament.
- Dub Side's follow-up, Dubber Side of the Moon (2010), featured remixes by international DJs and dub producers, pushing the reinterpretation even further into electronic territory.
- Countless jazz artists have tackled individual tracks—"Money" becomes a swing groove, "Breathe" an atmospheric ballad.

Each approach reaffirms the same truth:

Dark Side is not just a set of songs. It's a framework for reflection.

- In 1994, Pink Floyd themselves performed The Dark Side of the Moon in full during their Pulse concerts—a self-tribute of sorts, made more poignant by the band's looming disbandment.
- Roger Waters' solo tours from 2006 to 2008 brought a theatricality and political urgency to the performance—backed by multimedia visuals and modern relevance.
- In 2023, NASA commemorated the album's 50th anniversary by broadcasting it into space, beaming "Eclipse" towards a distant star. It wasn't a tribute by a band or a fan—it was a gesture from

Earth itself.

Covering Dark Side isn't just about paying homage. It's about grappling with it.

The album's themes remain as vital today as they were in 1973—fear, time, mortality, madness, greed, alienation. Whether it's through dub, metal, jazz, or electronica, artists keep coming back to this record because it offers a mirror—and each genre reflects something different.

It dares artists to ask:

- What would this sound like if we had written it?
- What truths can we reveal in these familiar shapes?
- Can we find ourselves inside it?

The answer, again and again, is yes.

The Dark Side of the Moon doesn't just accept reinterpretation.

It demands it.

Because it was never meant to be fixed in time.

It was meant to orbit—forever adapting, forever reflecting.

CHAPTER TWENTY-SEVEN
THE WIZARD OF OZ THEORY – COINCIDENCE OR CONNECTION?

The urban legend that never dies

It's one of the most enduring myths in rock history. A rumor passed from college dorm rooms to internet forums, whispered in record stores, and immortalized in late-night experiments:

If you play Pink Floyd's The Dark Side of the Moon while watching The Wizard of Oz, they sync.

The idea seems absurd—Pink Floyd, a 1970s progressive rock band, secretly crafting a psychedelic alternate soundtrack to a 1939 Hollywood musical? And yet… try it, and strange things happen. Dorothy balances on a fence as the alarm clocks of "Time" explode. "The Great Gig in the Sky" swells as the tornado hits Kansas. Lyrics like "balanced on the biggest wave" seem to narrate onscreen events with eerie precision.

It's called "The Dark Side of the Rainbow."

But is it real?

Or just the product of collective imagination, cosmic coincidence, and the strange human need to find meaning in synchronicity?

The theory first gained major traction in the mid-1990s, thanks to internet message boards and fan zines. The steps were precise:

1. Start The Dark Side of the Moon on the third roar of the MGM lion.
2. Mute The Wizard of Oz and watch as uncanny overlaps unfold.

With the rise of DVDs and CD players—both allowing precise timing—the theory spread like wildfire. Pink Floyd fans, stoners, students, and skeptics all tried it. And many were convinced.

Not just by one or two coincidences—but by dozens.

It felt too perfect to ignore.

Pink Floyd, for their part, have categorically denied any intentional connection.

- David Gilmour called it "a complete load of hogwash."
- Nick Mason suggested it was "American radio guys having a laugh."
- Roger Waters, never one to shy away from meaning, dismissed it as "bulls***."

No one in the band—or anyone involved in the production—has ever claimed it was intentional. They weren't even aware of the theory until decades after the album's release. And frankly, syncing a 43-minute album to a 101-minute film, across multiple reel changes, seems technically impossible—especially in the analog 1970s.

Still… the legend lives on.

There's something irresistible about The Dark Side of the Moon colliding with The Wizard of Oz—two cultural juggernauts, both surreal, both concerned with illusion, journey, and transformation. One is a black-and-white-to-Technicolor fantasy about finding your way home. The other is a swirling meditation on madness and mortality.

The theory thrives not because it's true, but because it feels true.

Psychologists would call it apophenia—the tendency to perceive patterns where none exist. But maybe it's more than that. Maybe it's a testament to how deeply immersive and emotionally resonant Dark Side is.

It's an album so powerful, it makes anything feel like it's unfolding to its rhythm.

Even Oz.

Today, fans continue to host Dark Side of the Rainbow screenings—at college events, indie theaters, even in sync-ready YouTube videos. Whether believers or skeptics, audiences lean in, gasp, and marvel at how the visuals seem to align:

- Dorothy opening the door to Technicolor just as "Money" kicks in.
- "Brain Damage" coinciding with the Scarecrow's wobbly antics.
- "Eclipse" playing as Dorothy returns to Kansas.

It's performance art by accident.

And in a way, that's exactly what makes it magical.

Ultimately, the answer may not matter.

Whether or not Pink Floyd intended any connection is almost irrelevant. What matters is how the theory captures our desire to find hidden meaning, to uncover layers of experience, to connect art across time and genre.

The Wizard of Oz theory endures because The Dark Side of the Moon invites mystery. It's an album steeped in the unknown—time, madness, death—and what better companion to it than a dreamlike fable about a girl far from home?

Maybe it's a prank.
Maybe it's a myth.
Maybe it's just the universe having fun.

But one thing's for sure:

There's no place like Dark Side.

CHAPTER TWENTY-EIGHT
DARK SIDE IN FILM, TV, AND POP CULTURE

The album's influence beyond the record player

Some albums are confined to headphones.
The Dark Side of the Moon escaped the stereo and entered the collective imagination.

Its influence isn't just musical—it's cultural. For over five decades, Dark Side has seeped into film scenes, TV montages, documentaries, advertisements, memes, and even psychological studies. It became the shorthand for anything deep, trippy, introspective, or unsettling. Like Kubrick's 2001 or Dalí's surrealist paintings, Dark Side became a visual metaphor—a reference point for the unexplainable.

This wasn't just an album people listened to.

It became something people quoted, sampled, parodied, revered, and feared.

Even without licensing, Dark Side has shaped the sound design of hundreds of scenes. Its fingerprints are everywhere in cinema and television:

- The haunting heartbeat from "Speak to Me" has been echoed in countless horror trailers and psychological thrillers.
- "Time" has been referenced in films dealing with aging, regret, or mortality—its clock motif now universal shorthand for existential urgency.
- "The Great Gig in the Sky," with its wordless howl of anguish, has inspired sound designers across horror and sci-fi genres, from Black Mirror to Stranger Things.

Although official syncs of the album in mainstream film are rare—due to the band's tight licensing control—the mood, pacing, and psychological weight of Dark Side became a stylistic influence, especially on directors from the 1980s onward.

The prism-and-rainbow cover alone became one of the most replicated images in history—seen on:

- T-shirts
- Posters
- Skateboards
- Tattoos
- Coffee mugs
- iPhone cases
- Dorm walls around the world

It became more than a cover. It became a symbol—of mystery, intellect, rebellion, taste, and timelessness. When characters in movies or TV shows are meant to be deep or slightly unhinged, there's often a Dark Side poster on their wall.

Notable examples include:

- The Simpsons, which has referenced Pink Floyd and Dark Side on multiple occasions, often with surreal flair.
- Rick and Morty, with its dimension-bending tone, clearly owes a debt to Floyd's vision of fragmented reality.
- That '70s Show, where Dark Side is played for humor and atmosphere, but always with affection.
- Doctor Who, Stranger Things, Freaks and Geeks, and Euphoria have all evoked Floydian themes visually or narratively.

One of the reasons Dark Side retains its mythic aura in pop culture is because Pink Floyd never sold out. The band famously refused to license the album to advertising. There's no soda commercial with "Money," no car commercial with "Time." In an age when rock music is regularly chopped and sold, Floyd's decision to protect the mystique only added to its allure.

The result? When the album does appear—even just referenced or sampled—it feels consecrated.

Artists from nearly every genre have paid tribute to or sampled Dark Side:

- The Weeknd cited Dark Side as an influence on the cinematic

sound of After Hours.
- Kanye West has drawn on its concept-album structure.
- Radiohead, Tool, and Tame Impala have all nodded to Floyd's sonic layering and conceptual ambition.

Electronic and hip-hop producers have long sampled its ambient textures, despite copyright hurdles. "On the Run" has been chopped into breakbeats. "Us and Them" has been used to score spoken-word segments in podcasts and experimental videos.

The album became part of the language of audio-visual media.

In the internet age, Dark Side found new life as meme fuel:

- The Wizard of Oz sync theory sparked hundreds of remix videos and fan-made mashups.
- "Comfortably Numb" (from The Wall, but often misattributed) is often conflated with Dark Side material, adding to its mythic sprawl.
- TikTok and YouTube creators now use clips from the album as background for spiritual rants, ASMR sessions, or psychedelic "journey" videos.

Even outside its original context, Dark Side became cultural shorthand for altered perception, existential dread, and emotional depth.

In an era of algorithmic playlists and disposable hits, The Dark Side of the Moon has become a badge of real musical listening. Referencing it in media implies depth. Showing it on screen suggests complexity. To love Dark Side is to align oneself with a lineage of seekers, thinkers, and feelers.

It's not just music anymore.

It's a mood. A myth. A marker in the pop-cultural subconscious.

CHAPTER TWENTY-NINE
PHILOSOPHY AND PSYCHEDELIA –
INTERPRETATIONS AND THEORIES

Existentialism, consciousness, and listener analysis

The Dark Side of the Moon is not just an album.

It is a philosophical mirror.

Like the prism on its cover, it refracts human experience into its most elemental themes—time, madness, death, greed, conflict—and invites listeners not only to hear them but to live inside them. It's not a concept album in the sense of telling a story. It's something more elusive and ambitious:

A musical philosophy of being.

The record became a soundtrack not to events, but to the inner life. And over the years, scholars, fans, psychologists, mystics, and acid-tripping philosophers have all asked the same question:

What is The Dark Side of the Moon really trying to say?

From its opening heartbeat to its final note of "Eclipse," the album functions as a meditation on existence itself. Roger Waters' lyrics are rooted in existentialism, particularly the kind explored by Camus and Sartre:

- We are thrown into a world we didn't choose.
- Time slips away, unnoticed, until it's too late.
- Death is not a fear—it's an inevitability.
- Sanity is a fragile social agreement.
- Greed is a shared madness.

In this light, Dark Side becomes a sonic essay on the absurd condition of modern life. It doesn't offer answers. It offers questions dressed in melody and echo.

"And you run and you run to catch up with the sun, but it's sinking…"

That's not a lyric. That's existential despair, condensed.

While Pink Floyd had moved beyond the overt psychedelia of Piper at the Gates of Dawn, the experience of Dark Side remained deeply psychedelic—just not in the kaleidoscopic, technicolor way. It's a psychedelia of the mind, not the eyes.

- "On the Run" mimics a panic attack, anxiety in sound.
- "Time" conjures the expanding and collapsing of memory.
- "Us and Them" induces a kind of dissociative empathy.
- "The Great Gig in the Sky" lifts the listener out of language entirely.

It is music designed not just to entertain, but to alter perception. With or without drugs, the album creates the sensation of moving through thought.

This is what makes it timeless—not tied to LSD or '70s mysticism, but to something much older: the human need to explore what lies behind the veil of ordinary life.

More than most albums, The Dark Side of the Moon invites projection. Each listener hears themselves in it. Some interpret it as a critique of capitalism. Others see it as a journey through the chakras. Some hear a spiritual rebirth. Others feel a descent into madness.

And none of them are wrong.

Because the brilliance of Dark Side is its open architecture—a carefully composed structure that allows for infinite meaning. The lyrics are sparse. The music is evocative. The spaces in between are where the listener lives.

It is not an album you decode.
It is an album that decodes you.

Psychologists have drawn comparisons between Dark Side and the work of Carl Jung—especially the idea of the shadow self. Jung argued that every person harbors a hidden self, made of repressed fears, desires, and truths. To become whole, we must confront that shadow.

That confrontation is what Dark Side stages musically:

- "Speak to Me" is birth.
- "Time" is realization.
- "Brain Damage" is confrontation with the self.
- "Eclipse" is the reckoning.

The final line, "There is no dark side of the moon really… it's all dark," suggests not nihilism—but acceptance.

We are all shadows.
And that's okay.

Dark Side is not a religious album. But it feels spiritual. It's about transcendence without dogma, awakening without preaching. It speaks not of gods, but of consciousness—of looking inward and realizing just how little time we have.

It resonates with Buddhists and atheists alike. With Christians, Taoists, agnostics, and seekers of all kinds. Because what it's really doing is reminding us:

You are alive.
You are afraid.
You are temporary.
And you are not alone.

In the end, The Dark Side of the Moon doesn't tell us what to believe.

It reminds us to ask.

And that's why, 50 years on, we're still listening.

CHAPTER THIRTY
50 YEARS LATER – DOES IT STILL HOLD UP?

Reappraisal by critics, fans, and scholars

Time is the great equalizer. It erases hype, silences marketing, and dims the glow of even the brightest moments. And yet, some albums don't fade—they intensify.

The Dark Side of the Moon is one of them.

Fifty years after its release in March 1973, it no longer needs defending. It is beyond genre. Beyond generation. Beyond debate. The real question now isn't how great it was, but:

Why does it still feel so necessary?

Initial reviews were respectful, if not always awestruck. Rolling Stone praised its ambition but stopped short of calling it a masterpiece. Some critics found the album too polished, too cerebral, too bleak.

Today, the tone is different. Reissue reviews, retrospectives, and academic essays uniformly praise the album as a pinnacle of recorded music. Pitchfork gave its 30th anniversary reissue a perfect 10. Mojo and Uncut rank it alongside Sgt. Pepper, Pet Sounds, and Highway 61 Revisited as the most influential records of all time.

What changed?

Critics, like everyone else, had time to live with the record. And with each passing decade, its themes only deepened—aging, mortality, greed, mental health, the speed of modern life.

What once felt like a studio experiment now reads as prophecy.

Unlike many classic rock albums, Dark Side didn't become a dusty relic for aging boomers. Instead, it grew younger. In every generation, it finds a new audience—teenagers discovering vinyl, college students staring at ceilings, musicians learning how to listen.

Its endurance among fans isn't based on nostalgia. It's based on relevance.

- Gen X heard the ticking clocks in the age of cubicles.
- Millennials heard the chaos of capitalism in "Money."
- Gen Z hears the anxiety in "On the Run" and sees their own mental health struggles reflected in "Brain Damage."

It doesn't matter what year you're born.

You get to Dark Side eventually.

Today, The Dark Side of the Moon is dissected not just in music magazines, but in university syllabi. It is studied in courses on:

- Music production and engineering (thanks to Alan Parsons' meticulous design)
- Philosophy and existentialism (via Roger Waters' lyrics)
- Cultural studies (as a lens into post-war British alienation)
- Psychology (through its portrayal of madness and emotional suppression)

What was once dismissed as stoner music is now examined with the same seriousness as Beethoven, Coltrane, or The Beatles.

Why?

Because it asks enduring questions in an unforgettable format.

Because it still sounds like the future.

Many 1970s albums feel dated—trapped in analog mud or lyrical naivety. But Dark Side is startlingly modern. Its sound design, pacing, and spatial awareness rival anything made in Pro Tools.

Put on headphones in 2025, and:

- The heartbeat still pulses in your chest.

- Clare Torry's voice still rips your soul open.
- Gilmour's guitar still cuts through time itself.

It doesn't just hold up.

It holds you.

Perhaps the most remarkable thing about The Dark Side of the Moon in the 2020s is this:

It's an album about the dangers of speed, disconnection, distraction—and here we are, five decades later, more distracted and disconnected than ever.

We've built a society on notifications, gig economy panic, curated identities, and attention debt. And this album—recorded on 16-track tape in the early '70s—still cuts through all of it.

It slows you down. It makes you listen. It reminds you you're alive.

That's not nostalgia.
That's relevance.

In the end, the question "Does it still hold up?" feels almost absurd.

Because The Dark Side of the Moon doesn't live in the past.

It lives in us.

CHAPTER THIRTY-ONE
WATERS VS. GILMOUR – CREATIVE TENSIONS

Collaboration, conflict, and artistic friction

Great art rarely comes easy. And The Dark Side of the Moon is no exception.

Behind the seamless production and conceptual unity lies a story of rival visions, creative chemistry, and a collision of egos. It was the beginning of one of rock's most famous—and ultimately fracturing—partnerships: Roger Waters vs. David Gilmour.

Their tension didn't ruin the album.

It powered it.

Like positive and negative charges in a battery, their opposing energies created the spark that lit the whole thing.

By 1973, Pink Floyd had evolved from a Syd Barrett–led psychedelic group into a more structured and sophisticated force. And at the center of that transformation were two distinct personalities:

- Roger Waters: bassist, lyricist, and conceptual architect. Cerebral. Intense. Political. He thought in themes and arcs—he saw albums like novels or films.
- David Gilmour: guitarist and sonic craftsman. Melodic. Intuitive. Emotional. He spoke through texture, phrasing, and feel.

Waters wrote the words. Gilmour made them soar.

And when they worked together—as they did on Dark Side—the results were staggering.

Although The Dark Side of the Moon is often framed as a Roger Waters vision, the truth is more collaborative. Waters certainly set the thematic tone—life, death, time, money, madness—but Gilmour was instrumental in shaping the sound world of the album.

- It was Gilmour who co-wrote "Breathe," "Time," "Us and Them," and "Any Colour You Like."
- His guitar solos—especially on "Time" and "Money"—became essential emotional anchors.
- He co-produced the album alongside Waters and the rest of the band.
- And he championed sonic experimentation, including the use of synthesizers, soundscapes, and textures that gave the album its futuristic feel.

Yet tension simmered beneath the surface. Waters was increasingly taking the reins, eager to guide the band's trajectory with a clearer narrative hand. Gilmour, while often more reserved in interviews, pushed back when he felt the music risked being overshadowed by message.

This creative friction was not yet open warfare—but it was brewing.

In hindsight, Dark Side represents the perfect equilibrium between Waters' brain and Gilmour's heart.

Waters brought meaning.
Gilmour brought beauty.
Neither would have made the album work alone.

Their disagreements, though real, were productive—focused on what served the album best, not who would get the credit.

Nick Mason recalled that while sessions could get tense, especially when editing transitions or finalizing mixes, there was still a sense of collective purpose. The vision came first.

But that balance wouldn't last forever.

After Dark Side, Waters' dominance grew. By Animals and The Wall, he was the primary creative force—writing most of the lyrics, dictating themes, and making executive decisions about arrangements, mixes, and even which members would perform on which tracks.

Gilmour increasingly found himself fighting for space—not just sonically, but artistically.

The fallout was slow but seismic:

- Creative disagreements during The Wall sessions.
- Bitter arguments over the use of session musicians.
- Personal distance growing during tours.
- And by The Final Cut (1983), the band had become, in essence, Roger Waters with a supporting cast.

Waters left Pink Floyd in 1985, believing the band could not—and should not—continue without him.

Gilmour disagreed.

Under Gilmour's leadership, Floyd released A Momentary Lapse of Reason (1987) and The Division Bell (1994), achieving massive success without Waters. Waters, meanwhile, pursued a solo career steeped in politics and concept-heavy albums like Amused to Death.

The feud grew public and acrimonious. Legal battles. Press jabs. Decades of silence.

And yet, their legacy remained intertwined.

In 2005, fans witnessed the unthinkable: the surviving members of Pink Floyd—including Waters—reunited for Live 8, performing together for the first time in over two decades.

For one night, the animosity faded. The music won.

And while a full reunion never materialized, that performance reminded the world what they could achieve when united.

In later years, both men expressed a measure of respect, if not full reconciliation. They acknowledged each other's genius—even if they still bristled at the past.

In the end, the Waters vs. Gilmour story is not a footnote to Dark Side.

It's part of its DNA.

The friction didn't break the album—it built it. Their competing visions created something neither could have made alone. Their arguments pushed boundaries. Their disagreements carved out a masterpiece.

They were not friends.

They were forces.

CHAPTER THIRTY-TWO
HOW THE ALBUM CHANGED PINK FLOYD FOREVER

Fame, expectations, and future directions

Before The Dark Side of the Moon, Pink Floyd were respected.
After it, they were mythic.

The album didn't just change rock history. It rewired the band's destiny.
It elevated them from experimental outliers to global icons—and, in doing so, reshaped their sound, their identity, and their internal dynamics forever.

It wasn't just a career breakthrough.
It was a point of no return.

In the late 1960s and early '70s, Pink Floyd had carved out a loyal following on the strength of their live shows, their spacey improvisations, and albums like A Saucerful of Secrets, Ummagumma, and Meddle. They were ambitious, but not chart-toppers. They were underground royalty, not pop stars.

Then came Dark Side—and everything changed.

- Sold-out stadiums replaced intimate auditoriums.
- Private creative sessions became global press events.
- The avant-garde experimenters became the standard-bearers of album-oriented rock.

The fame was not just immense. It was all-consuming.

Success came with pressure. The Dark Side of the Moon set a creative benchmark so high, it haunted everything that followed.

"How do you follow perfection?"
"How do you top a cultural monolith?"

The band quickly realized that they could not repeat Dark Side—nor did they want to. But the weight of its success became a creative burden, a measuring stick for every chord, concept, and concert.

The result? Albums became more ambitious, more intricate—and often darker.

- Wish You Were Here (1975) was a meditation on absence and disillusionment, with the ghost of Syd Barrett looming.
- Animals (1977) was angrier and more political, fueled by Waters' growing dominance.
- The Wall (1979) was a full-blown rock opera about isolation, trauma, and ego, as the band fractured around it.

The themes of Dark Side didn't end—they intensified.

With fame came friction. As Dark Side elevated the band, it also elevated the stakes. Creative disagreements—once minor—became major. Artistic differences widened. Roles changed:

- Roger Waters emerged as the primary conceptual force.
- David Gilmour fought to preserve musicality and balance.
- Rick Wright, increasingly sidelined, would eventually be fired during The Wall sessions.
- Nick Mason, ever the steady hand, remained neutral—but weary.

The unity that defined Dark Side was slowly dissolving, replaced by creative silos and power struggles.

Ironically, the very album that proved the power of collaboration also planted the seeds of division.

The Dark Side of the Moon cast a long shadow—not just over Pink Floyd's music, but over their sense of identity. They were no longer just musicians. They were mythmakers, symbols of existential rock, bearers of generational angst.

They couldn't go back to being a band.

They were now a brand, a phenomenon, a benchmark.

This brought opportunity—and exhaustion.

- The band increasingly leaned on spectacle.
- Tours grew theatrical, massive, and alienating.
- Personal lives suffered. Friendships frayed.
- By 1985, Pink Floyd as it once existed was effectively over.

Despite all the strain, the album gave them something invaluable: immortality. It allowed them to explore Wish You Were Here, Animals, and The Wall without commercial fear. It gave them the platform to chase vision over radio play.

And though the classic lineup would never fully reunite, Dark Side remained the thread that bound them.

- Gilmour continued to perform "Time" and "Breathe" with reverence.
- Waters brought the album on tour in full decades later, turning it into modern theater.
- Even Rick Wright, long gone from the spotlight, was brought back into the fold on The Division Bell, as a nod to what once was.

In the final reckoning, The Dark Side of the Moon made Pink Floyd legends.

But it also made them fragile.

It proved they could craft sonic masterpieces—but showed how human they really were.

CHAPTER THIRTY-THREE
THE DARK SIDE OF SUCCESS – PERSONAL STRUGGLES

Pressure, egos, and what came next

For all its beauty and balance, The Dark Side of the Moon came at a price.

Its success was colossal, but so was its fallout. Behind the acclaim, the money, and the myth, Pink Floyd were grappling with something more insidious: the psychological cost of making—and then living inside—the most perfect album of their lives.

Fame wasn't freeing.

It was fracturing.

Once Dark Side became a phenomenon, every decision that followed came with a new gravity. Creative freedom became creative paralysis. Every chord, every lyric, every studio session carried the invisible question:

"Is this as good?"

This constant self-comparison stoked insecurity, control issues, and creative domination. Roger Waters, increasingly feeling like the guardian of the band's legacy, began to tighten his grip. What had been collaboration was becoming directive.

And David Gilmour, whose melodic sensibility had helped define the record's soul, was growing frustrated.

The once democratic band was becoming Waters' vehicle.

Rick Wright, Pink Floyd's atmospheric architect, was among the first to suffer. Despite his essential contributions to Dark Side, he found himself gradually sidelined.

- On Animals, his presence faded into the mix.
- By The Wall, Waters wanted him out entirely.
- Wright was fired during recording—but hired back as a salaried musician for the tour.

He went from co-creator to contractor in the band he helped build.

Wright's struggles weren't just professional. He battled depression and substance abuse in the years that followed. His quiet demeanor was misread as disinterest. But it was grief—the slow mourning of being erased from something he loved.

Roger Waters bore the weight of the band's conceptual ambition. But with that burden came isolation. As he took on more creative control, he distanced himself emotionally from the rest of the band.

Waters wasn't just writing about madness—he was living on its edge. His obsession with control, his perfectionism, and his desire to push boundaries brought masterpieces like The Wall and The Final Cut—but at the cost of camaraderie.

By 1985, he had left the band, believing Pink Floyd should end with him.

The split wasn't just musical.

It was spiritual.

David Gilmour's struggles were quieter but no less real. Known for his calm demeanor and soaring solos, Gilmour found himself unwillingly thrust into leadership after Waters' departure.

He carried the Floyd name forward, but always with the shadow of Dark Side behind him. Critics questioned whether the band without Waters had legitimacy. Fans wondered who the "real" Pink Floyd was.

Gilmour responded the only way he knew how: with music.

The Division Bell (1994) and A Momentary Lapse of Reason (1987) were personal and spacious, but they couldn't escape the comparison. Even Gilmour himself admitted that the weight of history was hard to bear.

Nick Mason, the ever-steady drummer, remained neutral—publicly, at least. But even he struggled with the band's internal implosion. Though he contributed less to songwriting, he was emotionally invested in the idea of Pink Floyd as a brotherhood.

That brotherhood had splintered.

And with each legal battle, press jab, and public silence, Mason watched a legacy become a battlefield.

In the years following Dark Side, the band members—together or apart—never stopped grappling with what it meant.

It wasn't just an album.

It was a life event.

- Waters, in solo interviews, continued to circle the themes of death, isolation, and madness.
- Gilmour, in his later work, returned to themes of time, regret, and reflection.
- Wright, until his death in 2008, quietly returned to his roots with soulful solo work.
- Mason, now the custodian of the band's story, remains the connective tissue—carrying the history into a new century with respect and care.

Pink Floyd's story is not unique in its arc—from harmony to hubris, from unity to estrangement. But Dark Side of the Moon made that journey more intense.

Because few bands ever created something so universally embraced, yet so personally destabilizing.

It gave them everything they dreamed of.

And everything they feared.

CHAPTER THIRTY-FOUR
THE WALL BEFORE THE WALL – SEEDS OF LATER MASTERWORKS

How Dark Side laid the path to Wish You Were Here and The Wall

In hindsight, The Dark Side of the Moon was never just an isolated marvel.
It was a launchpad.
A blueprint.
A psychological and sonic excavation that foreshadowed everything to come.

When Pink Floyd made Dark Side, they cracked open the human condition. But they hadn't yet explored what lay beneath that condition—absence, disillusionment, and the slow decay of identity. These were the emotional undercurrents that would swell and break across their next two masterworks: Wish You Were Here and The Wall.

The band didn't pivot after Dark Side.
They descended deeper.

Roger Waters once said that the success of Dark Side gave him the confidence to dig deeper into personal themes. Where Dark Side mapped existential terrain—time, money, death, madness—Wish You Were Here turned its gaze inward toward loss and estrangement. And The Wall? That was the implosion.

But the roots of both lie in Dark Side:

- "Brain Damage" and "Eclipse" introduced psychological fracture, foreshadowing the disintegrating psyche of The Wall's Pink.
- "Time" and "Us and Them" addressed the futility of modern life, an existential thread that runs directly into the numb isolation of Wish You Were Here.
- Even the heartbeat that opens and closes the album suggests a lifeline—one that would later be cut off entirely in The Wall.

If Dark Side was the diagnosis,
Wish You Were Here was the grief.
The Wall was the breakdown.

While Dark Side is lush, cohesive, and meditative, it's not just an endpoint—it introduced musical signatures that carried forward:

- Seamless transitions between tracks became a Floyd hallmark.
- The use of recurring motifs—like the heartbeat or laughter—prefigured the sonic callbacks in The Wall.
- The band's embrace of synths and tape loops, pioneered in "On the Run," evolved into the sound collages of The Wall's "The Trial" or Wish You Were Here's machine-driven alienation.

It was on Dark Side that Pink Floyd learned to make albums as cinematic experiences. That language would only become more sophisticated.

Dark Side marks the true emergence of Roger Waters as a thematic leader.

Though the music was still collaboratively created, the album's lyrics bore Waters' fingerprints—introspective, biting, socially critical. This voice would become more assertive and more autobiographical on the next records.

- Wish You Were Here mourns Syd Barrett and indicts the music industry.
- Animals channels Orwellian rage at society's class structures.
- The Wall becomes an operatic reckoning with Waters' own trauma.

It all began with Dark Side—where Waters found his voice not just as a bassist, but as a narrative force.

For all its polish and cohesion, Dark Side also marks the beginning of divergence within the band.

- Gilmour's musical sensibilities favored emotional feel and melody.

- Waters began gravitating toward structure, ideology, and control.

That split, subtle on Dark Side, becomes definitive by The Wall. But even on Dark Side, the tension served the music.

By Wish You Were Here, the friction was more evident.

By Animals, it was caustic.

By The Wall, it had become the story itself.

There's a haunting symmetry to Pink Floyd's golden trilogy:

- Dark Side listens to the ticking clock.
- Wish You Were Here mourns the moments we missed.
- The Wall traps us behind everything we failed to express.

Each builds upon the last, but Dark Side is where the emotional architecture was first sketched out. It gave Pink Floyd permission to create albums not just of music, but of philosophy, grief, and confrontation.

They didn't just ask what does it mean to live?
They asked how do you survive it?

CHAPTER THIRTY-FIVE
FINAL REFLECTIONS – WHY THE DARK SIDE OF THE MOON ENDURES

A summing up of the album's eternal mystique and impact

Some albums are hits. Some are milestones.
And then, once in a rare while, an album becomes something more—
a mirror,
a myth,
a companion to the soul.

The Dark Side of the Moon is that rare work of art.
It doesn't merely survive the passage of time.
It defines it.

From its first heartbeat to its final eclipse, the album has offered every listener something deeply personal—and yet universally shared. It's not an album you outgrow. It's one you grow into.

Why does it endure?

Because it was never about 1973.

The album's themes—mortality, madness, greed, time, empathy—are not tethered to a cultural moment. They're embedded in the human condition. Whether you're hearing it on vinyl in a candlelit room or streaming it through headphones on a city train, The Dark Side of the Moon still speaks.

It doesn't tell you what to feel.
It gives you space to feel.

Its technical achievements alone would be enough to cement its status:

- Seamless track transitions
- Pioneering use of tape loops and synthesizers
- Immaculate production by Alan Parsons and the band

- A cover design so iconic it's now a language of its own

But Dark Side isn't merely the sum of its parts.
It's what those parts evoke.
A feeling.
A sense of being suspended between the infinite and the intimate.

Few albums carry such emotional architecture. It begins with chaos ("Speak to Me"), slides into calm ("Breathe"), races through anxiety ("On the Run"), confronts the march of time, descends into wordless emotion, critiques capitalism, mourns division, and ends with madness and a fleeting glimpse of unity.

It's less a collection of songs than a cycle of revelation.

It listens like life itself.

From Radiohead to Kendrick Lamar, Muse to Nine Inch Nails, the influence of Dark Side runs like an underground river through modern music. Not simply in sound, but in spirit.

It gave permission to be ambitious.
To make albums as statements, not just singles.

For listeners, it became a rite of passage—passed between generations like a treasured book or whispered secret.

- The first time you hear "Time" at the exact right moment in your life.
- The ache of "Us and Them" during personal or political turmoil.
- The chilling beauty of "The Great Gig in the Sky" when you can't find words.

These are shared sacred experiences.

Most art tries to capture a moment.
Dark Side captured being.

It's not timeless because of its sounds or sales. It's timeless because of its truth.

- We age.
- We lose.
- We fear.
- We hope.
- And in the end, we're all just trying to make sense of what it means to be here.

Roger Waters, David Gilmour, Rick Wright, and Nick Mason didn't set out to write a universal scripture. But that's what they created—music that feels like it was waiting for you, no matter when you find it.

At the end of the album, after the music fades, there's a voice:

"There is no dark side of the moon really…
matter of fact, it's all dark."

It's a whisper of cosmic irony. A reminder that understanding is elusive. That life, like this record, doesn't hand you easy answers.

But within its grooves, millions have found clarity.

Not because it explained the world—
but because it held them while they tried to feel their way through it.

The Dark Side of the Moon endures because it doesn't try to shout over life's noise.
It listens with you.
And sometimes, that's enough to make sense of the silence.

Printed in Dunstable, United Kingdom